GW00793168

How to Write a Blog

By Scribendi.com

Print Edition

ISBN: 1492338605
ISBN-13: 978-1492338604

CONTENTS

1   Introduction   1

2   Part One: So You Want to Write a Blog   3

3   Part Two: Technology   10

4   Part Three: Doing the Research   45

5   Part Four: Time to Write   53

6   Part Five: A Blog Is For Life   78

7   Part Six: Getting It Read   85

8   Part Seven: Monetizing Your Blog   93

9   Bonus: Helpful Blogging Tools and Resources   99

10   Acknowledgments and Works Cited   115

SCRIBENDI

INTRODUCTION

Do you have something you want to say to the world?

Maybe you want to share your revolutionary ideas about the TV show *Friends.* Maybe you have a lot of funny cat pictures you think will make people laugh. Maybe you have a product you'd like to sell.

In its report on the State of the Blogosphere 2011, Technorati surveyed over 4,000 bloggers around the world. And that's just the number of bloggers who volunteered to take part—the very tip of the iceberg!

Well, how do you go about it?

Today, thousands of people worldwide use blogs to express their ideas and opinions or to promote products and services. Blogs are one of the most powerful tools available for communication and marketing purposes.

But, what *is* a blog?

Simply put, a blog is an online space. Moreover, a blog can be anything you want it to be: a place to share your favorite recipes, write reviews of new products, or even keep a personal journal. A blog is what you make it.

However, creating a unique and exciting blog requires planning, research, and a lot of work. It's worth it, though, to create a site you can be proud of, full of original content.

Before you jump in and start building your blog, consider the question we began this book with:

Do you have something to say to the world?

You do? Good. Now, ask yourself a few more questions:

- **WHAT** do I want to say?

- **WHO** will want to read it?

- **WHY** should they care?

- **HOW** will I make them care?

- **WHEN** will I update my blog?

- **WHERE** will I host my blog online?

Don't worry if you can't answer all of these questions just yet! The purpose of this guide is to help you be clear about what your blogging goals are and how to meet them. You will learn how to go from the initial stages of creating your blog to the realms of building readership—even making a profit, if you wish.

Ready? Let's go!

PART ONE: SO YOU WANT TO WRITE A BLOG

Before you create your blog, there are decisions to be made. First, you need to decide on a topic and identify your target audience. Then, you must determine what *you* want from your blog, and establish some long-term goals. This may sound like a lot of work, but we're here to help make the process fun and rewarding!

Finding your niche

You may already have some idea of what you're going to write about, especially if you're planning to promote a particular product, business, or service. Even if this is the case, you still need to determine the specifics of your topic in order to make it truly unique. This is known as defining your blog's "niche."

The topic of your blog should be something you're passionate about and a subject you know very well. Readers will see right through you if you don't know your stuff. Successful blogs are made of authentic, compelling content.

Once you commit to writing a blog, it's time to begin creating content. Writing content takes constant work, but you don't want to turn the process of updating your blog into a chore! Writing posts should be something you enjoy, so think about what you find fun and interesting to explore.

If you're struggling to come up with a niche, try this exercise. Take three pieces of paper, and in the center of each write one of these headings:

- Topics I know a lot about

- Topics I feel passionate about

- Topics other people will want to read about

Explore these three factors and find topics that meet all three criteria. For example, you might know a lot about pool cleaning, and people may want to read about it, but you may not feel particularly passionate about it. On the other hand, you may feel passionately about your boyfriend, and know *everything* about him, but it's unlikely that the rest of the world will be interested in reading this information! (Your boyfriend might not be pleased, either.)

Once you've written down your headings, create a mind map of possible topics around each one. Look for topics that appear on all three pages. These are the potential niches for your blog. For each topic that meets all three criteria, ask yourself:

- Do I know enough about this topic to write convincingly about it?

- Do I feel excited about this topic? Do I think about it often?

- Could I write about this topic regularly without growing bored?

- Is it likely that there's a market for this topic and that other people will want to read about it?

- Am I able to write about this topic in a unique and interesting way?

Identifying your target audience

Once you have a niche you think your blog will fit into nicely, then you need to identify a target audience for your specialty.

Regardless of whether you're hoping to monetize your blog, the ultimate aim is to build an audience. Your blog needs to be as appealing for other people to read as it is fun (and challenging) for you to write.

What kind of people do you think will want to read your blog? Male or female? Young or old? Tech savvy or technophobic? How can you draw them in and keep them coming back for more? This is your target audience—the people who will become the core readership of your blog.

The most important part of blogging is learning to understand your audience. The nitty-gritty of how to build up a strong readership base is covered in Part Six. For now, you just need to identify your target audience, to help you design your blog and write posts.

For example, you may decide that you're targeting the fans of a theme, be it video games or gardening. But there are other factors to consider, especially in broad topic areas, because hundreds of other blogs already exist in the same niche. You could target a certain demographic, for example, girl gamers or older gardeners. Putting a unique spin on your topic will make your blog stand out.

Your choice of target audience will also affect multiple elements of your blog—particularly the tone of your writing. Your tone of voice when writing for teenagers, for example, should be different from the tone you adopt to appeal to older readers. Many writers and bloggers recommend that you write to one (real or imagined) person, who:

- Is a fan of your niche

- Is friendly, but will notice your mistakes

- You would enjoy spending time with

- Is eager to read

Writing to one person will help you focus and strengthen your voice so you can avoid that oh-so-common pitfall of trying to please everyone!

Your blog should cater directly to your target audience. They should be able to access your blog and think, "Wow! It's as if it was designed just for me."

If it helps, you could even find a picture of your ideal reader and stick it above your desk while you work, to act as a reminder that you're writing to just one person.

For fun or for profit?

While preparing to launch your blog, it is important to determine exactly what you hope to achieve. There are many possible motivations and goals for starting a blog.

Technorati divides the bloggers surveyed for the State of the Blogosphere 2011 report into five categories:

1. Hobbyists: these bloggers make up 61% of the blogosphere and report no income from their blogs.

2. Professional Part-timers: making up 13% of the blogosphere, these bloggers receive some compensation from blogging but do not consider it their full-time job.

3. Professional Full-timers: these bloggers make up just 5% of the blogosphere. They are independent bloggers who consider blogging to be their full-time job.

4. Corporates: corporate bloggers make up 8% of the blogosphere, blogging for the company for which they work.

5. Entrepreneurs: 13% of the blogosphere consists of entrepreneurs who blog for their own company or organization.

Now you should ask yourself which of the above categories you would like to join. Your niche is linked to the relative financial goal of your blog.

Long-term goals

"Impatience" is often listed as one of "The 7 Deadly Sins of Blogging."

Achieving your goals will take time. Remembering this will help you to stay committed to your blogging enterprise. When considering your long-term goals, it's important to consider your blog's lifespan. It's often assumed that bloggers begin without any thought for how long their blogs will last. Yet many blogs have built-in, or natural lifespans. For example, if you've started a blog to chart your weight-loss experience, or to follow the story of your three-month cruise, there will be a logical point (assuming all goes well) where your narrative comes to an end. Sometimes this is a good way into blogging. It takes the pressure off and gives you a chance to spend some time working on a simple hosted blog before launching a more serious, self-hosted blog that you may want to monetize.

It's also fine to leave the lifespan of your blog open and undecided. Just be aware of the direction and shape your blog begins to take, and make sure to re-evaluate your goals as you go along. If your blog begins to diverge on an unexpected tangent, do not feel like you have to rein it in! Be flexible! You may find that some of your initial goals become less important as new goals emerge.

Create your goals in a concrete way. They don't have to be overly ambitious; they should simply reflect what you want to get out of your blog as time goes by. Here are a few examples:

- **At two months:** I will have written 10 posts.

- **At six months:** I will have 100 RSS subscribers.

- **In one year:** I will begin to make money.

Long-term goals are important to help steer your blog along a successful path. Think of them as guideposts to keep you on track, rather than stress-inducing indicators of success.

Naming your blog

The name of your blog is more than what appears in the URL of your site—it is how readers come to identify you and your contributions to your niche. It is important to pick a name that is:

- **Original:** Your blog should stand out from others in your niche. On a practical basis, if your domain name is too similar to another site, your readers may end up in the wrong place.

- **Relevant:** Readers should be able to identify the niche of your blog from its name. Keywords are useful for immediately establishing your topic, but make sure the name is creative and interesting as well.

- **Understandable:** A vague name that consists solely of keywords will not reel them in. Clearly establish what your blog offers.

- **Memorable:** You want your readers to keep coming back, so make the name something they can remember. Snappy names are better than long ones; keep it simple.

- **Easy to type:** This may seem basic, but you'd be surprised how many people create blog URLs like "gam3r-c3ntra1" and then wonder why no one finds it! Readers will not bookmark your page straightaway, so they need to be able to remember what to search for when they come back for a second look.

The name of your blog will also be displayed as the header of each page on your site. The name should be striking and memorable, like a book title. No matter what post your readers are looking at (or what page a new reader lands on), the header will always be there.

If you're struggling to come up with a good name, you can draw inspiration from other blogs in your niche. Take a look at these examples:

- **Copyblogger**: Features articles on copywriting and blogging, hence the use of the two terms in the name.

- **Problogger:** Provides advice and information for professional bloggers and shows this in its name, using a similar technique to Copyblogger.

- **Fuel Your Blogging:** Part of the "Fuel Your Brand" network, which has several "fuel your _____" sites.

Note how the name of each of these sites contains the keyword "blog," but also finds a way to communicate the specificity of its interests.

Think of naming your blog as being like getting a tattoo: it's something that's going to stay with you for a very long time, so pick a name that really speaks about who you are and that you will not find embarrassing a few years down the line!

PART TWO: TECHNOLOGY

Thanks to different blog platforms and hosting options, there's a method of blogging to suit any level of technical ability.

Blog platforms and hosting

A blog platform is a system, online or in downloadable software, that allows you to create and manage your blog. Choosing a suitable platform at the outset can help you to achieve your blogging goals, whether or not you decide to spend money at this stage. Making the right choice depends on three main factors:

- **Goals:** How seriously will you take your blogging? If you're looking for a casual hobby or want to take time coming to grips with the blogosphere, you will not want to spend money on a self-hosted platform with a custom domain. If you want to develop your brand or business, however, you'll need to invest to make a profit.

- **Time:** How often will you update? Again, there's no point spending money on a blog you're going to update once every couple of weeks. If you'll be posting more frequently, it might be worth the added expense.

- **Budget:** How much are you willing to spend? Be realistic.

Annual blogging costs can add up if you opt for a paid self-hosted platform with a custom domain and any premium features you may purchase to enhance your blog.

The main decision is whether to choose a hosted or self-hosted platform. Let's go over the important features of each platform:

Hosted

Hosted blog platforms are simple to use and often free. These platforms host your blog on their domain, so you do not have the added expense of a third-party host. The catch is that you will be subject to the platform's URL formation system, consisting of two elements: the name you choose for your blog, and the platform's extension. Alternatively, some hosted platforms *do* allow you to buy a custom URL while still using their platform and domain.

Hosted platforms also give you access to a number of default templates with a degree of customization. When using these options, creating a post is as simple as filling in a few fields and pressing the "publish" button.

Another big advantage to using a hosted platform is that you do not have to worry about installing updates manually. Everything is managed online and therefore updated automatically. Finally, using a hosted platform will give your blog an immediate boost in search engine rankings, because the domain that's hosting you will already have a high level of visitors.

Self-hosted

Self-hosted blog platforms offer a higher level of creative control than hosted platforms. However, to take full advantage of this, you need to understand how to tweak your site's code. Basic knowledge of CSS and HTML is invaluable, although you can always use a professional web designer. Self-hosted platforms are adaptable, and the range of customizable layouts and plugins is constantly expanding.

Having your own URL makes your blog more professional and memorable, but setting up a self-hosted blog is complicated. You'll need to download and install software, arrange hosting, establish databases, upload to a server, and more. In addition, a self-hosted blog platform is labor intensive and entails ongoing annual costs and updates that have to be installed manually.

While hosted and self-hosted are the two basic types of blog platforms, there are many others offering a combination of features. To get a better idea of what's available, let's go over the features of six of the most popular blog platforms—three hosted and three self-hosted, with a quick start guide for each type of service.

Hosted

WordPress.com

WordPress.com is a free blogging platform. One of the most popular hosted platforms, WordPress is feature rich and incredibly simple to work with—great for newbie bloggers. It has many basic themes, traffic statistics, anti-spam filters, and search engine optimization (SEO) tools. For a fee, you can also purchase premium themes and custom domains to enhance your blog.

When you first access WordPress.com, you'll hit the "Freshly Pressed" page. If your blog is featured on this page, it receives several days of free exposure and extra traffic. This is another great benefit of WordPress; it is a huge community of over 40 million bloggers. Getting help blogging on WordPress is easy, as there are thousands of third-party guides and tutorials as well as official support.

Quick Start

Get started at www.wordpress.com. Here you have the option to create a new account by following the link in the top right corner that says **"Get started here."** You can investigate the site first via the **"Learn more"** link. When you're ready, you'll be taken to a simple form requesting some basic info.

1. The first and most important field is the address for your blog. If you want, you can just create a username at first, which will allow you to view and follow all of the WordPress blogs. You can create your own blog later on.

2. Your default blog address will be **www.yourblogname.wordpress.com**, which will not cost a penny. Alternatively, you can buy a custom domain name straightaway. You can begin with the WordPress default address and upgrade to a custom domain later if you wish.

3. The domain name you choose must be original. If you type in a blog address that's already taken, the box will turn red and a red cross will appear. If you pick an address that doesn't exist yet, you'll see a green tick instead.

4. Next, you'll choose a username and password. Other bloggers will see your username on your WordPress profile. Follow the instructions to the right of the page to make sure your username and password meet all of the requirements. Next, enter your e-mail address. This is the address where your activation e-mail will be sent. You need to activate your account to move forward, so type your address carefully.

5. Below this field is a check box to follow the WordPress blog. This is recommended to keep up-to-date on new themes, features, and other news. You can also choose from over 100 different languages to blog in.

6. Before moving on, you'll be offered the WordPress Value Bundle. Although it's a free platform, WordPress also offers paid upgrades.

7. Remember to check out the WordPress terms of service. By submitting your details, you're agreeing to these conditions, and your activation e-mail will then be dispatched. You'll need the link in this message to access your blog, but while you're waiting, you'll be directed to a page where you can fill in some basic info for your WordPress profile.

8. If you haven't received your e-mail, check the bottom of the current WordPress page to make sure you typed your address correctly, and update it if necessary. Once received, click the link in the e-mail to access your blog reader, a personalized WordPress location that allows you to find friends, view the blogs you follow, see recommended blogs, posts you've liked, and review blogs by topic. Later you can also use the tabs to view notifications, blog stats, and more.

9. To start working on your blog, click the **"My Blog"** tab. Your blog should be visible here, labeled as primary. Below is the option to create a new blog, which you may want to do at a later stage. You can choose which blog is primary if you have multiple blogs.

10. Click the "**Dashboard**" tab below your blog's name. You'll be redirected to your dashboard, which is the hub of your blog, visible only to you. This is where you'll perform all the main tasks on your blog, such as changing its appearance and publishing posts. The first time you visit your dashboard you'll be greeted with a big welcome from WordPress, with links to helpful resources and an introductory video.

With these tools, you will be able to pick a theme, start customizing, and compose your first blog post! For more information and detailed guides about creating and maintaining blogs on WordPress.com, visit the platform's comprehensive support site.

Blogger

Like WordPress.com, Google's Blogger offers free use of its platform, a domain name, and hosting. To create a Blogger blog, you need to login using a Google account. If you do not have an account already, you'll need to sign up.

Thanks to Google's ownership, blogging on Blogger gives you access to many great features, including integration with Google tools like Analytics and AdSense, which help to keep track of your blog statistics and make money. Themes on Blogger are called templates, and the Template Designer user interface allows customization no matter what template you choose. You can even test out the Template Designer before joining Blogger.

Quick Start

1. Get started at www.blogger.com. You'll be greeted by a simple Google account sign-in page, where you'll need to log in to continue. If you already use a Google service like Gmail or Google Groups then you'll already have an account, so type in your details. If not, look for the red button in the top right-hand corner of the screen that says "**Sign Up**."

2. Creating a Google account is easy. You'll be directed to a basic form with all the standard fields: your name, your chosen username (which will also become the body of your @gmail.com e-mail address), and a few other bits of information. Look out for the tick boxes; you'll need to agree to Google's terms and conditions, and you'll also have the chance to set Google as your homepage and allow Google to use your details to personalize content and ads.

3. Next, you'll be taken through a couple more pages before you're redirected back to Blogger. The first will tell you about your Google profile; you can customize it now or go back to it later. Then you'll be reminded of your account details and will see the **"Back to Blogger"** button.

4. Now that you're logged in, you'll need to choose whether you want to use your Google+ profile or a different username on your blog. If you choose the latter, you'll need to click **"Create a limited Blogger profile."** This means you will create a mini-account under a different name or pseudonym. You'll still use your Google account to blog, but users will not see that your Blogger profile is linked to your Google+ account.

5. The next page is your Blogger dashboard, which has two main sections. At the top will be a list of your blogs, currently empty. Below you'll find your Blogger reading list, where you can save other blogs that you enjoy. You can also switch views to access your favorite blogs through Google Reader. You'll notice you're automatically following the

Google BuzzFeed blog, which is a useful source of info on Google services.

6. To create your first blog, click the **"New Blog"** button. A pop-up window will appear asking for your blog's title and domain name. The domain name you create at this point will be: **www.yourblogname.blogspot.com** as you won't be able to add a custom domain until later. If the domain name you want isn't available, a yellow exclamation mark will appear next to the input box. If it *is* available, you'll see a blue tick instead.

7. You'll be asked to choose a template for your blog from a small selection.

8. You'll now be redirected back to your Blogger dashboard, where your new blog should be waiting for you. You can view the blog straightaway, and you'll be prompted to create your first post. You can click this prompt, or the button with a white pencil on an orange background. Both will take you to the Blogger post editor—a simple interface where you can add text, images, and other media to create blog posts.

Now your blog is up and running and you're off to a great start. For help and assistance with the next stages of your blog on Blogger, such as customizing your templates, visit the Google support center.

Typepad

Typepad is the most advanced of the hosted platforms. It offers tiered pricing plans to suit your budget and blogging goals. The unlimited plan is the most popular, which offers access to the site's templates, personal support, and domain mapping, as well as the ability to create an unlimited number of blogs and custom design elements.

Typepad is a popular platform for serious bloggers who do not want the extra hassle of a self-hosted blog. You can create a professional-looking blog on Typepad, with complete customizability, if you know what you're doing. For the beginning blogger, Typepad offers Power Launch and Blog Tune-Up services, where Typepad's team will review, assess, and help improve your blog. There's also a free version of Typepad called Typepad Micro, but this is an extremely basic platform that is very limited in customization and design features.

Quick Start

1. The URL for Typepad is www.typepad.com, where you'll find a friendly homepage on a green background. You can explore the Typepad community before signing up by following the links on this page. When you're ready to get started on your blog, click the big orange button that says **"Start Now | 14 Day Free Trial."**

2. You'll be directed to a page that asks you to choose one of the three tiered pricing plans. At this stage, you may only be interested in the free trial, but you still have to pick a pricing plan. If you do not cancel your subscription when your trial expires, this is the plan you'll automatically be charged for. The basic set-up process is the same no matter which plan you choose.

3. Next, you'll need to fill in your details, starting with your blog's URL. Initially, your domain name has to be **www.yourblogname.typepad.com**, but you can set up a custom domain later. If you type in an available URL, a green tick will appear. An unavailable URL will provoke a small notification below the entry field. Other required info is standard: enter your e-mail address and create a password and display name.

4. Typepad is the only hosted platform that requests financial information, though you will not be charged until your free trial expires. You can cancel your trial at any time.

5. Typepad offers a 15% annual discount if you pay for a whole year's membership in advance. You can also enter promotional codes to get a discount. You'll then need to enter your billing information and address.

6. When you're ready, hit **"Sign Up,"** and be aware that by doing so you're agreeing to the site's Terms of Service and Privacy Policy, which can be viewed by following the links above the final submission button.

7. Now that your account is created, you can start working on your blog. You'll also notice links to other Typepad blogs at the bottom of the page, offering inspiration from the Typepad blog showcase. When you're ready to write, click **"Get Started."**

8. You'll be redirected to the Typepad dashboard, where all of your blog activity is controlled. Posting to your new blog is easy; you can take advantage of Typepad's quick post field to publish a note, photo, or video; or you can click the link that reads **"Write a full post"** to access Typepad's rich-text editor.

Now that you're set up on Typepad, you're ready to begin customizing your blog with themes and designs; also visit Typepad's dedicated customer center, which features blogs, tips, and advice from the Typepad community.

Self-hosted

WordPress.org

WordPress.org's open source software provides flexibility and customization. Downloading and installing WordPress is free, so the only paid elements are your domain name and hosting fees. Once you purchase these, you'll then have access to loads of interesting and dynamic themes, plugins, and an easy-to-use dashboard that makes posting to your blog as simple as on a hosted platform.

Setting up WordPress can be tricky, though you can find a detailed tutorial on its web site. Alternatively, you could choose a host provider that offers 1-click WordPress installation. WordPress currently recommends Bluehost, DreamHost, and Laughing Squid. Installing and running self-hosted blog software like WordPress is not for the beginner, as you need knowledge of SQL databases, FTP clients, and HTML/CSS coding.

Quick Start
1. Before installing WordPress, you need a domain name and host. We

recommend using a host that offers integrated 1-click installation of the WordPress software.

2. If you do choose a host with 1-click installation, it will usually be performed on the host's site. If it isn't, you'll need to visit www.wordpress.org, download the software, and then install it manually. Use the help resources on the WordPress web site as your guide.

3. Once the installation is complete, you'll need to go to your site using the domain name you registered. You should be greeted by the WordPress welcome screen.

4. The welcome screen will ask you to create a title for your blog, a username, and a password. You'll also need to add your e-mail address correctly, because this is the address WordPress will use to send you important information, such as alerts about new comments and password reminders. There's also a check box to choose whether you'd like your blog to be listed in search engines, such as Google and Technorati. All of this information can be changed at a later stage in your blog's administration panels.

5. Once these details are confirmed, you'll be taken to your WordPress dashboard, which is similar to the dashboard for a WordPress.com hosted blog, except the self-hosted version has a range of additional options and tools. Along the left side is the navigation bar, where you can select different aspects of your blog to format and edit. Whatever you click on will appear in the main window to the right.

6. Creating your first post is easy. Click the **"Posts"** tab on the left to work on a new entry. WordPress's text editor is simple to use, and you can switch tabs to work with either rich text or HTML.

7. You can preview your blog at any time by clicking on the blog's name, which is displayed in the upper left corner.

8. When you want to return to your blog, visit

www.yourblogname.com/wp-admin.php. You'll be met with a login screen, and then redirected to your dashboard.

For additional help and support many third-party resources are available online, as well as the official WordPress codex, which is a huge store of information.

Drupal

Drupal is a highly rated open-source content management system that can be used to create blogs. Once you've completed a basic Drupal installation, you can create any web site you want. Drupal is well known for its flexibility, with thousands of modules you can add to the core software to enhance your site.

Unfortunately, Drupal is also difficult to install. It uses a building block system, and though the core software comes with a selection of themes and modules, you will probably want more. If you have a specific type of blog in mind, Drupal recommends many distributions that provide features and functions for different kinds of sites in one single download. This means you can quickly establish the site you want, rather than wasting time installing and configuring individual elements.

Quick Start

1. As with the other self-hosted platforms, you need to have a domain name and a web host set up before you download and install Drupal software. Like WordPress, Drupal recommends several hosts that are well integrated with the Drupal community and offer quick installs, including Bluehost, and InMotion Hosting.

2. If your chosen host doesn't offer a Drupal install, you'll need to download the Drupal software directly from its web site at www.drupal.org. For manual installation, check out the installation guide for step-by-step instructions.

3. Alternatively, you could go straight to a Drupal distribution and install a full-site package. These packages contain the Drupal core software, contributed modules, themes, and a pre-defined configuration.

4. One important step in the installation process is running the installation script within your web browser. Then, you will reach a page titled **"Configure Site."** Here you can give your site a title and enter an e-mail address that will be used to send out automated messages from your Drupal site.

5. In the site maintenance account section, type a username, e-mail address, and password. You will also need to select your country and time zone, and decide whether to opt in for automatic updates and e-mail notifications, which is recommended for keeping your site's security up to date.

6. Next, you will be informed that your Drupal installation is complete, and that you can click to visit your new site. You should then see your homepage, and your administrator account will be automatically logged in. A black administration toolbar should be displayed across the top of the page, from where you can create content, edit your profile, manage your Drupal installation, and do much more.

7. Before you start posting, you need to enable your Drupal site as a blog. Go to the **"Modules"** tab and check the box next to the blog module, which is in the core Drupal installation.

8. Access the **"Content"** tab to create your first blog entry.

9. When you want to return to your Drupal dashboard after logging out, visit **www.yourblogname.com/user**. You will see the login fields that will direct you to your blog, with the administration toolbar at the top of the page.

Drupal is one of the trickier platforms to manage. However, many printed publications are dedicated to the use of Drupal. A list of these, along with other tools (such as official documentation, help forums, and training services) can be found in the support section of the Drupal web site.

SCRIBENDI

Movable Type

Movable Type is considered by many to be the most "serious" blogging platform. Created by a husband and wife team who wanted a better blogging tool, Movable Type is an extremely powerful platform. Its main strength is its huge range of features and plugins, which allow you to create a unique blog. Code tweaking provides near complete customizability.

Movable Type may be a powerhouse platform, but it's not easy to install or simple to use. If you're not familiar with uploading files to a web server, this isn't the platform for you.

Quick Start

1. First, you will need a domain name and web host. Movable Type recommends that you check out its server requirements carefully to make sure that your chosen host fits the bill. Otherwise, you may find that your host and platform are incompatible.

2. Movable Type does a lot of the installation work for you, but it can still be a tricky process. Some hosts offer automatic installs of Movable Type, such as A2 Hosting and TMDHosting. Alternatively, you can download the version of Movable Type software that suits your needs from www.movabletype.com.

3. Moreover, remember to choose a version that matches your goals as a blogger. The open-source software is designed as a platform that developers can build upon, extend, and customize. The Movable Type Pro packages are focused more on the blogger or business than the developer, while the Advanced package is recommended for major enterprises. Details about the different versions of Movable Type software can be found on its web site.

4. If you're having trouble installing Movable Type, the developer community at www.movabletype.org offers a handy installation guide. If you're willing to pay, you can purchase the official Movable Type Installation Service from After6 Services, to make your life easier.

5. Once your chosen version of the Movable Type software has been installed, you will need to set up your blog. Access your Movable Type control panel by typing your domain name into the URL bar of your web browser, followed by a forward slash and the name of the directory in which your blog administration files are stored. You will then see a login screen where you can type in your blog username and password.

6. Your username should be visible in the top right-hand corner. From here, you can create, maintain, and manage multiple blogs (even the free personal edition allows you to create up to three different blogs). You can also add new posts and begin to customize your blog's appearance and settings.

For more information about setting up and maintaining blogs using Movable Type, seek out the extensive support documentation offered by the developer community; its forums are also helpful. If you need more solid support, you can purchase a Movable Type Pro license with its software and receive 12 months of support free, or you can purchase the package from After6 Services, depending on your license type.

Hosting and domain names

If you have chosen to go with the self-hosted option, you will need to find a hosting provider as well as a blog platform. You'll pay this provider an annual fee to host your blog on its domain. Most hosts will also allow you to purchase a domain name through them (recommended). Alternatively, you can purchase a domain name through a third party and then register it with your host.

Here are three of the most popular integrated hosting providers:

Bluehost

Bluehost is one of the most popular hosting sites. It provides solid support services 24 hours a day via phone, instant messaging, and e-mail. You can "try before you buy" through the Bluehost demo site, which allows access to various tools and features. Bluehost's comprehensive packages offer great value for bloggers on any budget, with unlimited domain hosting.

Go Daddy

Go Daddy offers hosting suitable for any size of blog, and it consistently offers discount deals on a variety of packages. Over 53 million domains have been registered with Go Daddy. It offers fast, secure, reliable hosting, and you can easily transfer your blog from another domain with no risk of losing your established content.

Host Gator

Host Gator offers a variety of different services, including shared, dedicated, and reseller hosting packages. Its easy templates and tools can suit both beginning bloggers and those requiring larger, more advanced sites. Host Gator has built a good reputation for reliability and support services and offers a 45-day money back guarantee on hosting packages.

Note: You do not have to self-host in order to have a custom domain name: WordPress.com, Blogger, and Typepad all allow you to buy a custom domain name and continue to host on their domain using their platform.

Layout and design

Although content is your foundation, an effective layout (theme, template, or skin that you choose) helps to strengthen a blog's appeal and enhance your blog's appearance.

Christopher Rice compares the overall aesthetic of your blog to mise-en-scène in film. Mise-en-scène refers to all the individual elements filmmakers use to construct their scenes, from the obvious, such as an antique armchair in which a character sits, to the seemingly trivial, like the white lace doilies on the coffee table. Every element is carefully considered, no matter how small, and they all work together to clearly establish location, time, and atmosphere. The design elements of your blog should similarly work to create the desired effect.

Header

The header is the first and most prominent design element readers see on your blog. No matter what page is being viewed, the header is always visible.

In most themes, the header contains the title of your blog along with a short tagline. The tagline should be relevant to your niche and could be literal, or a clever play on words. Take these two examples:

- FAIL Blog: Funny FAIL Pictures and Videos: this is a very literal tagline that simply explains the content of the site.

- Perez Hilton: Celebrity Juice, Not From Concentrate: Perez Hilton is a celebrity gossip site, and this tagline plays with the idea of "juicy" gossip.

Although some themes allow you to add other features to your header, this isn't an area you want to overcrowd; loads of ads and links are off-putting. Use an appropriate font and color to depict your niche and your own personal style.

Two features that *can* be effective when embedded in the header are social networking buttons (if they are a reasonable size) and a site search bar.

Sidebar

A blog's sidebar is usually a hub of activity, where you'll find most of the widgets and other useful tools. On a basic blog, the sidebar is usually vertical along the right-hand side; however, some themes place the sidebar down the left-hand side, along both sides, or contain no sidebar. Choose a layout that best suits your blog's aesthetic.

Like the header, the sidebar will appear in the same format on every page of your blog. Place the most important links and icons at the very top of the sidebar, since that gets the most attention from readers;

social networking icons, subscription buttons, certain ads, and/or a link to the sales page for your products or services go on this sidebar. Each platform offers a wide selection of plugins, and if you're using self-hosted software, you can download and install plugins. However, add only those that will be of genuine use to your readers and avoid overcrowding your page. Here are a few examples of tools you can add to your blog's sidebar:

- Photo gallery, with arrows to scroll through images

- Audio player, to play your favorite tunes to readers

- Blog archive, so readers can view your past blog posts by date

- Most popular posts, to show off your most-read content

- Countdown timer, counting down to a milestone or event

Footer

The footer is the area at the very bottom of your blog. On most platforms, the footer automatically displays information about your platform and theme. Typically, you can also add widgets to the footer in the same way that you would add them to the sidebar. However, the bottom of the page is an area less likely to be seen by readers, so carefully consider what you choose to place here.

Body

The body of your blog is the main area where posts are displayed. You can alter how your posts appear to suit your blogging style. For example, if you write very long posts, you may prefer the body of your blog to display only a sample of each recent post. If your posts focus on images, you may want a layout that prominently displays the featured images alongside headlines, rather than taking up space with text.

Navigation

The navigation elements of your blog allow readers to explore beyond the arrival point of the first page. Navigation tools can be incorporated into different areas of your blog layout, depending on your theme. Here are the main navigation methods:

- **Search bar:** Readers like search bars because they help locate exactly what they're looking for without having to sift through other content.

- **Categories:** If you're organized and sort your blog posts into categories, you can display the category list somewhere—such as the sidebar. Don't use too many categories, though, as this can get confusing. If you're pressed for space, you could display your categories as a drop-down list or word cloud.

Above is a word cloud created on Wordle.net. Clouds are a more interesting way to display categories or tags on your blog. The words are displayed in different sizes according to how often they were used. Similarly, in blogging word clouds, categories with lots of posts would be bigger than those with few, while frequently used tags will be bigger than those used less often.

- **Archives:** An archive of your blog posts allows readers to delve back into earlier content. Although blogs are constantly updated with new posts, connecting readers with your older material will help increase your site's stats and search engine rankings.

- **Post calendar:** A post calendar highlights the days of the month on which you published a post. This is a visually appealing alternative to an archive, although post titles aren't displayed, leading to confusion if you publish multiple posts on one day.

- **Popular posts:** A list of popular posts can be useful once your blog is established and has a decent number of posts to draw from. Popular posts can be calculated in different ways, such as number of page views, top-rated, or most liked. You could even install a plugin that shows posts that have been shared or liked by many people on Facebook and Twitter.

These are all methods that help readers navigate your blog. Your platform may also allow you to create fixed pages, which are extra pages you can use on your site to display information. For example, it's standard to have an **"About"** page or a **"Contact"** page. However, such pages should be easy to access, so consider including them in your navigation plans.

Static elements
Static elements are parts of the page that stay in the same location even when the viewer scrolls down. The blog by designer Doug Neiner, for example, has a static left-hand sidebar that includes a picture of him, contact information, and important social networking and related links.

Blogs that feature many posts on the front page can be extremely long, requiring a lot of scrolling to get all the way to the bottom. A static header or sidebar means your readers do not have to scroll all the way back up to the top to access certain links, thereby making it easier for them to continue their exploration of your site.

Colors and fonts
Colors can be powerful in provoking particular moods or attitudes, possibly owing to pre-established connotations with colors. A light pastel color scheme may suit a blog about toys and clothes, for example, whereas a blog about vampires might be better off with the tried and true combination of red, black, and white. Be careful to coordinate, and be selective: pick two or three colors that are associated with your niche and work with them, perhaps varying the shades to add texture, but remain within your chosen palette.

The font you choose needs to be clear and easy to read, otherwise your blog might as well be in a foreign language. If you use the same font for your blog's title, headlines, and posts, make sure it looks good in three different sizes. If you choose to use different fonts, make sure they all look good together on the page. Finally, choose a font that's appropriate for the tone of your niche and your writing. A serious news blog will be undermined if you use a font that dots the letter "i" with a love heart!

Themes, templates, and skins

Themes are basic structural design frameworks for blogs, and each of the major platforms approaches them in a slightly different way.

Here's a quick rundown on where you can find themes for all six platforms.

WordPress.com

Themes for a hosted blog on WordPress.com are accessed through your blog's dashboard. Select **"Appearance"** from the left-hand menu, then **"Themes."** The theme gallery will appear in the right-hand window. Here, you can view available themes in random order, sorted alphabetically, from newest to oldest, or from most to least popular, as well as premium themes, or themes developed by WordPress associates and partners. Use the search bar to find themes using particular keywords.

The theme view allows you to see a screenshot of the theme in action, with its name and other options listed below. Free themes will be available to **"Activate"** while premium themes will show an option to **"Purchase"** followed by the theme's price. You can view each theme fully by clicking **"Live Preview"** to see exactly what your blog's current settings would look like were the theme applied. Most themes allow some customization.

Blogger

Themes on Blogger are called templates. When you set up your Blogger blog, you have the option to view the numerous potential themes. Access them by clicking the name of your blog on your Blogger dashboard. This will take you to your blog overview, and down the left-hand side, you'll see the word **"Template."** Click on it to launch the template viewer in the right-hand window. Blogger has far less to choose from than WordPress.com, but it offers a greater degree of customizability.

The top of the template gallery shows the theme you're currently using and gives you the option to customize. If you're tech savvy, you can also edit your blog's HTML code. You can change the color of the background, adjust the widths of different page elements, and change the fonts for different textual elements. Blogger also gives you the option to choose from a selection of different base layouts, no matter what your theme, so you can shift design elements around the page.

Typepad

Typepad themes form the very basis of your blog's design, which can then be used as a foundation for a unique look. Once you sign in to your Typepad account, you'll see a box dedicated to managing your blog on the right side of the page. Click on the link that says **"Design"** to access your blog's design dashboard. Your current design will be displayed at the top of the page, along with its theme. Below, you'll see a box that reads **"Create a new design"** and below that, a green button, **"Choose a theme..."** that will lead you to the theme gallery.

In the theme gallery, you can view or browse all of the themes under the following categories: Microblog, Personal, Professional, and Simple. When you click on a theme in the main gallery, it appears on the right-hand side with a list of features; you can then preview the theme as it would appear applied to your blog. Once you've chosen a theme to use, you can change elements like colors and content, and add custom CSS style definitions for your design.

WordPress.org

Of all the self-hosted platforms, WordPress.org has the highest number of custom and premium themes available—more than 1,500 free themes in the WordPress Themes Directory.

WordPress also recommends many different sites that provide custom themes on a commercial basis. Some also provide additional services, such as support and advice. A quick Google search of WordPress themes will render hundreds to choose from, although sticking with those WordPress recommends ensures good quality.

Drupal

Drupal themes have to be installed. They are designed to provide a base for extensive customization, rather than to be used as they are. You can install and use themes contributed by other Drupal users, or, if you're competent with the technology, you can create and contribute your own to the community. You can also create sub-themes from existing themes; sub-themes inherit the resources of the parent theme.

Themes on Drupal's official web site are probably the most reliable you will find, although they are not "official" themselves and therefore may not be optimized for your blog and its purpose. Other sites, such as ThemeShark, RocketTheme, and Template Monster, produce Drupal themes and offer them to users at a price.

Movable Type

Themes on Movable Type are slightly more complicated than those on other platforms; they are made of elements like templates, categories, and custom fields. Themes have to be installed in the same way you would install a plugin, and then applied to the relevant blog. Once you've installed a theme, visit the dashboard for your Movable Type blog, click **"Design"** and then **"Theme"** on the side menu. You'll see a list of themes you can choose to apply. The theme currently in use will be marked. Advanced users can create themes from scratch and then share them with other Movable Type members.

Widgets and plugins

Hosted blogs have a range of useful widgets, while self-hosted blogs offer a wide selection of plugins to install. Here are some of the most useful widgets, plugins, and extensions available for each of the major platforms.

WordPress.com

WordPress.com widgets can be found by accessing your blog's dashboard, clicking the **"Appearance"** tab and then selecting **"Widgets"** from the drop-down menu. The widgets gallery will be displayed in the main window, with available widgets displayed on the left, and boxes representing different areas of your site on the right. You can drag widgets from the main section, drop them into the desired area of your blog, and order them as you choose. Some widgets have customizable options that will appear once you add them.

Here are three popular WordPress.com widgets:

- **Author Grid:** This is a useful widget if your blog is collaborative or you feature frequent "guest posters" you wish to promote. The author grid displays a series of author avatar images that show who has contributed to your blog. You can alter the size of the images displayed, and choose whether to display all of the registered authors or just those who have posted.

- **Goodreads:** This widget connects with the web site, a virtual library or book club where you can keep track of books you've read, are reading, and plan to read. Accounts are free, and once you've created one you can sort your books into shelves. When you add this widget to your WordPress.com blog, you'll be asked to input your Goodreads numeric user ID and choose which of your shelves you'd like to display.

- **Milestone:** The milestone widget displays a countdown to a date and time of your choosing. Once you've added it to your blog, you can give the countdown event a title and a message to display when the big moment arrives.

Blogger

Blogger widgets are called gadgets. To add one to your blog, visit your dashboard and click the **"Layout"** tab. You'll then see a basic mockup of your blog's layout in the main window. On various parts of the page you'll see links that read **"Add a gadget."** Click one, and a pop-up will appear displaying the basic, featured, and most popular gadgets that are available. If you click **"More gadgets"** you'll see gadgets from third-party developers. You can add your own gadget here by inputting a unique URL.

Here are three of our favorite Blogger gadgets:

- **Event:** You can advertise and promote an upcoming event on your blog using this gadget. Readers can view details, see a map, indicate whether they will attend, and see who else is going. The Event gadget is also integrated with Google Calendar, so readers can add your event to their schedule with one click.

- **Support My Blog:** This gadget is the perfect tool if you're hoping to get a few donations toward your blog. It allows users to donate via Google Checkout, although you'll need to create a Google Wallet to use it. Simply sign in with your Google account and then fill in the relevant forms to obtain a Google Checkout Merchant ID. This is a safe and reliable way to receive donations.

- **Translate:** Using Google Translate, you can add a translation gadget that will translate the text of your blog into another language, making it accessible to readers all around the world.

Typepad

The Typepad versions of widgets are called **"Modules."** These are found under the **"Design"** and **"Content"** sub-sections of your blog overview.

You'll see a list of modules displayed in a small scrolling box in the center of the page. When you click on a module, its details and the option to add it to your blog appear to the right. The module will then appear in the sidebar of your blog in the sample layout, and you can move it around to change the order in which the modules appear.

Here are three of the most useful Typepad modules:

- **E-mail Address:** This adds a link to your e-mail address in your blog's sidebar. Its presence here shows that you are willing to be contacted, which increases the possibility of user feedback, guest post offers, and advice from other bloggers.

- **Embed Your Own HTML:** This is a useful module for those with relatively advanced knowledge of HTML coding. It allows you to add your own HTML, so you can create a widget or module, or introduce one you have found elsewhere on the net.

- **Your Photo Albums:** This module displays a list of all of your Typepad photo albums in the sidebar of your blog. It's a particularly useful tool for photography or art blogs, so you can easily link viewers to all of your other work.

WordPress.org

WordPress.org has an extensive plugin directory that can be accessed by visiting the homepage, then clicking the **"Plugins"** tab on the navigation bar. On the main plugin directory page, you can search for specific plugins, view popular tags, and see the featured, most popular, and newest plugins. With WordPress plugins, you can literally do whatever you want with your blog. The directory allows you to download, rate, and comment on each plugin you come across. Three extremely useful plugins to add to your WordPress.org blog are:

- **All in One SEO Pack:** This highly rated plugin is designed to optimize your blog for search engines by using a variety of different features. Most of these could be installed separately, but here they are featured in one big bundle, which includes support from Google Analytics and nonce security. Beginners can install the pack and let it work its magic; advanced users can tinker with the plugin to fine-tune pretty much everything.

- **Scribendi.com Editing and Proofreading Services:** Even the best blogger makes mistakes, and there are many bloggers out there who want to get their work read but aren't professional writers themselves. The Scribendi.com plugin allows you to have your work checked by professional editors, and your content can be looked over and delivered back to you quickly and efficiently.

- **Spam Free WordPress:** Spam comments are a huge pain for any blogger. Moderating and deleting them takes time, so this plugin takes the task out of your hands. Spam Free WordPress claims to block 100% of automated spam.

Drupal

Drupal extensions, also known as modules, are found on the Drupal web site under the **"Download & Extend"** tab. Drupal recommends that if you find a bug or have a suggestion, you should get involved and help work out the problem. You can also create and share your own modules. Here are three unique and useful modules for your Drupal blog:

- **CAPTCHA:** This tool makes sure the person accessing your content is human, and not a spam-generating robot! It requires readers to enter a unique, randomly generated combination of numbers and letters. You could use a CAPTCHA to moderate comment submission or restrict access to other areas of your site.

- **Printer, E-mail, and PDF Versions:** This is an extremely useful module if your site contains content that users will want to print and share (for example, recipes or other instructions). The module automatically generates three different versions of your text and provides links to each.

- **Views Slideshow:** This module allows you to create a slideshow of any content you want displayed. It's also fully customizable so you can change how your content looks and how viewers can access it.

Movable Type

Plugins for Movable Type aren't found on the main platform web site; they're on a secondary site dedicated to the Movable Type developer community. When you access the developer (.org) site, you'll see that **"Plugins"** is the first tab on the navigation bar. Here you can browse the Movable Type plugin directory, where you can search, browse by tag, or browse by category.

Here are three recommended plugins for your Movable Type blog:

- **Facebook Connect Commenters:** Allows readers to login and comment on your blog posts via their Facebook account. When they login, each Facebook user will generate a local user account with their Facebook name and profile picture displayed.

- **Joomsayer:** Allows you to display quotations in your blog posts in a visually appealing way, making them stand out from the rest of the text.

- **Media Manager:** Allows you to create and manage a list of media items, such as books, CDs, DVDs, or anything else you can think of. You can search Amazon.com in order to add new items to your list directly, and then publish the list on your blog.

Some popular blogs

It's great to be original, but there's nothing wrong with being inspired by the biggest and best in the blogging world. The following 20 blogs have all been featured on Technorati's Top 100 Blogs, although the list is updated daily, so their positions vary. We've included blogs from a range of niches operating on different platforms, so you can see each one in action.

The Huffington Post (Movable Type)

The Huffington Post is a well-respected news blog read by people all over the world. Its color scheme is reminiscent of a newspaper—black text on a white background. The only color on the page comes from the featured images and subject headings. Different colors represent each of its article categories, such as dark blue for politics and purple for business. The emphasis is on content; a continuous stream of articles and featured images is organized into orderly columns. The blog's title is simple and demands little attention, allowing readers to focus on the news stories that dominate the page.

TMZ (Crown Fusion)

TMZ is a celebrity gossip site, so bold and brash is the name of the game. The blog uses a flashy red, black, and white color scheme. The white background (and some white text) keeps the site from looking dark, and the only other colors on the page come from images and ads for TooFab, a subsidiary of TMZ. TooFab distinguishes itself from its parent by sporting a contrasting blue color scheme. TMZ ads are designed to blend in with the aesthetic of the page. Content is featured in a continuous feed that displays images and brief articles. The focus is on videos and other media rather than on text, which is appropriate because TMZ also has a companion TV series to promote.

L.A. Now (Typepad)

Like The Huffington Post, L.A. Now uses a basic black and white newspaper color scheme, appropriate for a blog subsidiary of the *Los Angeles Times*. The tagline beneath the blog title establishes that it is dedicated to local news with frequent updates. Posts are displayed in a continuous news feed down the left-hand side. Time stamps emphasize the "up-to-the-minute" focus of the blog. The page footer features a valuable **"if you just missed it"** section, important for a site that is continuously updated.

Jezebel (Gawker)

Jezebel's tagline reads **"Celebrity, Sex, Fashion for Women. Without Airbrushing."** The emphasis here is on gossipy news that is direct and to the point. The site acts as a major aggregator, gathering suitable content and providing links to the full stories on other web sites. The blog itself is dominated by a large featured image at the top of the page that shows the current hot topic. Like TMZ, Jezebel uses the color red to make a bold statement and to highlight certain page elements, like headings and source links. The left-hand feed is a reverse chronological archive of articles from the past couple of days, each with a time stamp that alternates with a number. The number represents page views and is joined by a little flame icon which shows how "hot" each article is.

Deadline (WordPress.org)

At the time of writing, Deadline was going all out to promote the Emmy Awards, with an extensive background ad, an expandable ad in the header, and another in the sidebar. As a TV and film industry blog, Deadline relies heavily on revenue from this campaign. The rest of the site is all business, emphasized by the inclusion of job ad links in the header and sidebar, which provides a service for visitors. Extensive navigational tools help visitors find content that interests them. The blog allows visitors to filter content according to the industry area they want to read about.

Kotaku (Gawker)

The layout of Kotaku and Jezebel are similar, as both use the Gawker blogging platform. The same flame icon is used alongside featured articles to indicate how popular they are. Like Jezebel, Kotaku introduces its content with a striking image at the top of the page. As a site dedicated to video games, visual elements are essential, so it uses a bright, vibrant pink and yellow color scheme to make the page visually attractive. Content is more detailed than the brief summaries and links on Jezebel. The right-hand feed features one prominent post, followed by several smaller samples. These are accompanied by links to the full story and other related content.

Venture Beat (WordPress.com)

Like TMZ and Jezebel, Venture Beat also uses a red and black color scheme. However, the effect is very different, thanks to the mediating presence of grey, which gives Venture Beat a professional, stylish feel suitable for an industry blog with the tagline: **"Tech. People. Money."** This is a blog that gets straight to the point, with several featured articles and many more in the main feed. The editor's picks at the top of the feed and the author links down the left-hand sidebar show an emphasis on the people behind the page. Venture Beat readers care about the writers and their credentials. The customization of the social media buttons at the top of the page, designed to fit in with the blog's color scheme, is also a nice touch.

Zero Hedge (Drupal)

Zero Hedge is a site that focuses on finance and politics, so its layout and design are appropriately matter-of-fact. There is very little to distract from the blog's posts. Any images are small and nondescript, and there's barely any use of color. Dark blue is used to differentiate between certain types of text, and the dominant colors are black and white. There's some use of bold text to highlight important points and arguments. While the ads clash with the main aesthetic of the site, this keeps them visually separate from the rest of the site.

Laughing Squid (WordPress.org)

Laughing Squid is quite a unique blog, with a focus on interesting art, culture, and technology. With a broad niche like this, it's important to establish a clear identity. The prominent placement of the site's logo in the top right corner contributes to this sense of strength. The color scheme is a distinctive combination of vibrant green on white and black. The blog features a widget in the sidebar dedicated to explaining the ideas behind Laughing Squid. Post titles are very specific, since the blog covers a range of diverse topics, so it's important to let readers know exactly what they're getting. When it comes to advertising, Laughing Squid devotes a prominent place in the sidebar to promoting its hosting service, on which it relies for revenue.

Joystiq (Blogsmith)

Joystiq is a gaming blog that, like Kotaku, needs to make a striking visual impression on its visitors. This is achieved through the use of the color orange for highlights on a black and white background. The category icons used in the header to represent different gaming platforms establish the site's niche, so readers can easily identify Joystiq's content. Joystiq also uses a dynamic space in the featured story bar that appears below the navigation menu; the advertised topic changes every few seconds to show a range of hot topics, each with a set of relevant links to pages on the site. Each post is also marked with many custom icons to indicate its subject; these are like tags, only more visually appealing and easier to pick out.

Daily Kos (Scoop)

The Daily Kos is a serious news site, but it focuses on opinion rather than fact, so it steers clear of an excessively newspaper-like layout. Like Joystiq, the Daily Kos uses orange as a highlight color to draw attention to certain areas of the page. It avoids an overly dramatic edge by using a neutral white background without any black areas. Each post's headline is detailed and literal, explaining the exact content of the story, and often revealing the attitude of the piece. The information is clearly presented with quotations and information from sources identified in grey boxes, highlighting controversial points. Discussion is a major focus of the Daily Kos, with emphasis on community and action. The sidebar gives prominent placing to articles that have received the most comments. A **"Discuss"** button at the end of each post also encourages readers to get involved.

Hit & Run (Diderot)

Hit & Run is an opinion blog, a subsidiary of reason.com. It focuses on the discussion of controversial issues, such as politics and civil liberties, but with a human edge. Orange is used minimally throughout the site to highlight important elements, such as the Hit & Run logo, which is shaped like a speech bubble, again emphasizing the blog's purpose. This is solidified by the reason.com tagline, **"free minds and free markets."**

The main feed is complemented by a feed in the right-hand sidebar listing all recent posts, and is updated frequently throughout the day, with some posts as often as 15 minutes apart. Each full post is displayed with related topics on the left to explore further, and individual sharing links are along the top. Having these links at the top of each post means readers do not have to scroll down to the bottom of the page, providing a much easier and more straightforward way to share on sites like Facebook and Twitter.

This isn't happiness (Tumblr)

This isn't happiness is a perfect example of the simplicity of Tumblr, and in particular, its suitability for showcasing images. This blog is a stylish, post-modern enterprise dedicated to **"art, photography, design & disappointment."** The melancholy color scheme fits in with this concept. The whole blog is minimalist in design and execution, with the blog name and tagline on the left remaining static when readers scroll down through the content. The right-hand sidebar features navigation and page links, as well as sharing options, which are given no special treatment. The content in the central feed is almost exclusively images, with very few text entries, if any. This blog really takes advantage of Tumblr as a platform to share images, ideas, and attitudes.

ReadWrite (Movable Type)

ReadWrite is a blog about the web. The red header immediately draws attention to the top of the page and the blog's title and logo, which stand out in white. The navigation links are located at the top of the page and are extremely simple, giving you four basic options to find your way around. At the top of the sidebar are subscribe and sharing links, small in size but identifiable by their distinct colors. The only other tool in the sidebar is the Facebook social plugin, which allows readers to login with their Facebook accounts to "Like" a post. The feed features only samples of all of the most recent articles, and there are no other widgets or lists on the blog to show recent and popular posts.

Bleeding Cool (WordPress.org)

Bleeding Cool is a blog dedicated to comic books, so the layout needs to be edgy and dramatic, hence the stark contrast of black and white with dark red thrown in for bold highlights. To get away from the newspaper feel, Bleeding Cool uses a unique font for the blog title in the header, which creates more of a hand drawn feel. The whole top half of the page features very little actual content, and there are even two relatively large ads close together. The blog looks natural and integrated, however, with the positioning of the four custom black and white icons at the corners of the header section. This gives the page balance and makes it look symmetrical, which is pleasing to the eye. The content is then divided into two columns; since comics are the blog's primary focus, they get one column to themselves. TV and film are secondary topics, so they share the right-hand column.

The Official Google Blog (Blogger)

Google's official blog uses Blogger. The feel of the blog is typically Google: minimalist and built around white, black, and grey, with a burst of color in the blog's title and header. The blog title is a static element that stays in place as you scroll down the page, a constant reminder of Google's presence. The layout is basic, with sharing links in the sidebar. Facebook is notably absent; they are a direct competitor of Google+, so not something they want to promote! The focus of the page is on the content, with very few distractions. The text and layout are simple, an aesthetic favored by Google. Images and videos are embedded in the posts to enhance and complement the text, but they do not appear elsewhere.

The White House Blog (Drupal)

It's extremely important for a blog from the White House to look official and professional. The color scheme here is predominantly white and blue, with an occasional splash of red to remind us of the U.S. flag, a mini image of which can be seen in the navigation bar. The use of a traditional serif font gives a classic feel, as does the subtle background at the top of the page which, when you look closely, resembles a curved element of classic architecture. The posts all have very literal headlines, and the authors are indicated with an image and a link to their profile on the left-hand side. This is important for a site delivering political news, as readers want reassurance about the credibility of the sources. The e-mail sign-up form cleverly plays on the backing of major political players, inviting readers to receive e-mail updates **"from President Obama and Senior Administration Officials."** The inclusion of a photo gallery near the top of the sidebar gives a human feel to what could otherwise come across as a faceless government site.

The Unofficial Apple Weblog (TUAW) (Blogsmith)

This blog may be unofficial, but it still closely imitates the design and style of Apple's products and web sites. The navigation bar will be extremely familiar to Mac users, as will the icons used to change the way readers view the content. The color scheme is trademark Apple, and like Google, they favor simplicity over complex designs and the excessive use of images. While the official Google blog has no need for ads, the unofficial Apple blog uses them for revenue. Like Joystiq, TUAW distinguishes its content by separating it by device—in this case Apple devices like the iPod, iPhone, etc. Posts are displayed as samples with featured images, but TUAW also has the great **"Quick look"** option, which allows you to view a whole post in a quickly loading pop-up rather than on a new web page. This is extremely convenient, as it's easier to just close the post and return to the main page without navigating away.

PopWatch (WordPress.com)

PopWatch is a subsidiary blog of the *Entertainment Weekly* web site that focuses on pop culture news. It's less gossipy than TMZ, but similarly uses a bright color to make a bold statement instantly, in this case via the hot pink of the blog's title. The most prominent position in the sidebar is given to an internal ad promoting the *Entertainment Weekly* magazine. Below that is a list of the latest news; the posts on this site are fast-moving and quickly updated, so a list like this lets you see what's currently trending and what you may have missed. The content feed on the left is text heavy, focusing on the content of the articles. A photo section in the sidebar compensates for this, and works to balance out the page. Sharing links are prominently placed to the side of each post, allowing you quick access to social media. This blog is notably missing the standard navigation bar; instead it has two drop-down menus for categories and archives beneath the blog title, a handy space saver.

PART THREE: DOING THE RESEARCH

Would you write an essay or a novel without first doing some research? Of course not! So why skip the research phase when writing a blog?

Research is essential to blogging. It helps you to understand your niche and target audience better, and allows you to tailor your blog's layout, tone, and content. Moreover, you'll need to continue to research the development of your niche, the shifting priorities of your audience, and the subject of each of your blog posts.

Do your research, and you will build a strong reputation as a reliable source, possibly even an authority, within your niche.

Keyword research

Keyword research is often linked to SEO, or search engine optimization, and this can be an intimidating concept for new bloggers. Both keyword research and SEO are a lot simpler than they seem (see the dedicated SEO section in Part Six).

It doesn't matter how well written and engaging your posts are if nobody can find them. People need to be linked to your blog via search engine results when they search for related keywords. To make this happen, you must ensure that search engines can easily identify the topic of your blog and each post title. This is what will stimulate traffic to your blog. Once readers arrive, your well-written and engaging content can convert them into dedicated readers.

First, you need to identify the words people are using to search for topics in your niche. If you run a canine welfare blog, using "hound" as a keyword means you will probably miss out on all the traffic the word "dog" receives. Keyword research helps you identify the language your target audience uses to talk about your topic. If you are using the same words or phrases they are to discuss a topic, they will feel more engaged with your content and will be more likely to visit your blog. Mark Twain said, "The difference between the right word and the almost right word is the difference between lightning and a lightning bug." Words are powerful; the right words are unstoppable! But, how do you discover the right words to use?

In the past, marketers underwent long processes of surveying consumers and collating results. But now, dedicated keyword research tools, available online, make modern keyword research simple. These tools work by analyzing the terms and phrases people type into search engines like Yahoo, Bing, and Google. They can show you how popular a word or phrase is at a given time compared to its popularity in the past. You can use the results to compare the popularity of one topic to another, including near-synonyms, like "hound" and "dog." A useful (and free!) resource for understanding keyword research is Copyblogger.com's five-part guide to Keyword Research for Web Writers and Content Producers.

For instance, Google AdWords has a great keyword research tool, and it offers limited access for free. More advanced tools and resources, including some functions of the Google Keyword Tool, require payment. There are both good and bad tools out there, so check out the resources section of this book for a list of useful examples.

The Google Keyword Tool is easy to use and will provide enough information to start optimizing your posts and headlines. If you become more serious about blogging further down the line, it may be worth investing in paid software that offers advanced features.

Remember, trends change, and so does the language people use. You should update your keyword research often. In the process, you may find inspiration for blog posts as you discover new terms and combinations people are actively searching for, or you may even be able to predict the development of your niche in the future!

Be sure to keep all your keyword research safe and accessible, as it will come in handy. You will see how as we move through this guide.

Checking out the competition

Always strive for originality, but don't shy away from doing a bit of blogger espionage. Use your keyword research to find sites within your niche. Take a look at the top results and thoroughly study any competing blogs in your area. See what topics they're writing about, and store the ideas for future reference. Note the way these bloggers write, and think about how you can write about similar topics in different and unique ways. Record the blogs you find; they'll also be useful later.

Many bloggers keep a "swipe file." This is a place, virtual or physical, where you store resources to inform and enhance your blogging. These could include good blog posts you strive to match, pictures that inspire you, or articles you can use as sources for your next post.

It's important that you learn to recognize what makes a blog post successful, and why. Don't just look at posts you enjoy: seek out posts that have been read and shared numerous times. Try looking at posts that appear on the front page of Digg, or that have received thousands of likes on Facebook. Try to identify what makes them effective. Think about the following factors:

- The language used to appeal to the audience.

- The length of the post.

- The use of images and other media.

- The post's headlines and subheadings.

- How the post is structured to form a cohesive whole.

If you're struggling to identify what makes a post effective, try looking at the comments. Readers will often single out details they find compelling. You can also look through the comments to see what readers *do not* like, so you can avoid making the same mistakes!

Finding inspiration

Inspiration is all around us, every day. At first glance, our daily lives may not seem all that thrilling, but to a good writer, an entertaining blog post exists within the material of ordinary routines.

One of the best ways for writers to find inspiration and improve their writing skills is to read. As you continue to identify and learn from effective writing techniques, try venturing into reading territory you have not explored before. Here are a few suggestions:

- **Newspapers:** Good journalism has a lot to teach a blogger. Journalists work with facts, time limits, and space constraints, so news articles are great examples of concise, detailed communication.

- **Magazines and other publications within your niche:** You've probably read widely within your own niche if it is in an area you have a keen interest in. Start reading with a more critical eye, paying careful attention to the language used by other bloggers.

- **Short stories and novels:** Fiction authors know how to hook an audience's attention and keep it over time. Reading novels, thrillers, or even trashy romances will help you understand how to engage your readers' attention. Short stories demonstrate how to communicate a message in limited time, space, and words.

- **Letters, diaries, and journals (but not your teenage daughter's):** Look for published collections of first-person writings. Generally speaking, if someone's private writings are considered interesting enough to be published, his or her voice is probably uniquely appealing. It can be helpful and inspiring to see how other people have utilized the first person.

- **Your own writing:** Read your work from the past, both published and unpublished. Read through your old diaries or the speech you wrote for your brother's wedding. As a blogger, the ability to critique your own writing is essential, as you will need to edit your posts (or have them edited) before you publish them.

Keep virtual and physical clipping files for material that inspires you. You can bookmark or photocopy articles in magazines, pages of books, blog posts, or notes and letters you receive. If a quotation or proverb catches your eye, jot it down in a notebook. Every writer should carry a notebook and a pen, and most smartphones and tablet devices also have note-taking apps. Programs like Evernote and Google Docs will instantly save whole web pages, images, and chunks of text. If you prefer "speaking your mind," try a speech recognition software program like Dragon NaturallySpeaking from Nuance, or use built-in voice memo software on your phone or computer.

Planning for the future

The point of all this research is to prepare you for what lies ahead. You may not mind having a folder stuffed with all kinds of info, without a clear file-naming system or sub-folders. If that works for you, great! In contrast, you may want to sort your research into an organized system. This will prove helpful when you delve back into these resources later.

Here are some possible categories you can use to file research:

- Inspiration

- Ideas for posts

- Sources to explore further

- Great writing samples

- Useful quotes and statistics

You may also find it useful to divide your research into separate topic areas within your niche. These topic areas could later become categories on your blog, and each post you create will fit into one. This will allow readers to navigate your content with ease. For example, if you write a video game blog, you may sort your research into categories according to gaming platforms:

- Handheld gaming

- Mobile gaming

- PC gaming

- Console gaming

- Gaming accessories

Deciding on style and tone

Blog posts aren't like college essays or work memos—they're an independent medium, and the medium is a major factor in determining the style and tone of your writing. Just as you wouldn't write a letter to your friend using the same language and tone as you'd use to write a proposal for your boss, your blog writing will be distinct from other forms of writing that you currently engage in.

The general rule of thumb (though this is a guideline, not a law!) is that blogs are conversational in tone. Your blog should develop an ongoing conversation between you and your readers.

Because blogging is more intimate, even corporate and business blogs will adopt a friendly, casual tone, to give the organization a human point of contact. Therefore, consumers feel like they are interacting with a real person rather than a faceless corporation. While corporate blogs may remain slightly more formal than personal ones (including fewer personal experiences and anecdotes, and more technical language), their purpose is the same as non-corporate blogs: to build a community of readers.

The best way to gain loyal readers is to talk to them openly and honestly. Excessive formality can make readers uncomfortable and posts difficult and sometimes boring to read. In this age of scanning and skim-reading, readers will simply leave a blog where the posts take too much time and effort to understand.

Here are some other important tips about tone in a blog post:

- Avoid specialist terminology and complicated vocabulary, unless you are targeting a very specific audience you know will understand it (and you aren't concerned about alienating those who do not). If you're using words that *you* do not use in real life, chances are they're words your readers will not use or understand. No one will read a post they need a dictionary to decipher. If it is necessary to include specialist terms, include definitions to make things easier on your readers.

- Be friendly! You're trying to start a conversation with people, so you want them to feel comfortable. Try to be the person that everyone wants to talk to at a party—pleasant, and able to get along with anybody and everybody.

- Remember that it's not all about you, even if it is your blog. Posts that are overly egocentric will alienate readers. This doesn't mean you should never talk about yourself, but imagine you're participating in a real conversation when you do. No one likes that person who's all "me, me, me."

- Inject some humor into your writing. Getting people to smile or laugh makes them more likely to remember your blog. Evoking a positive emotional reaction enhances your readers' experience, lifting the words from the page into their own emotional realm.

- Finally, do not try too hard! Readers can tell if you're forcing something and it will make them uncomfortable.

Incorporating all of these elements into your writing will take practice. Style and tone should feel natural, but at first you may find it difficult to avoid sounding contrived. The more you write, the more natural your voice will become, and before you know it, you'll be the life of the blogosphere party.

PART FOUR: TIME TO WRITE

By now, your blog has a niche, a name, and a place in the blogosphere. What does it need next? Content, of course!

A blog is nothing without content. Some bloggers write extensive, essay-length posts, while others prefer short, pithy posts. Some blogs focus on images, while others are text heavy. Whatever your style and focus, the most important thing is to get cracking on some killer content that will start attracting readers. This way, you will be armed to confront every blogger's worst nightmare: the dreaded first post.

The dreaded first post

The first post on your blog is *more* than important! It's the first thing you publish and contribute to the blogosphere. It's written in *your* voice, with *your* name on it, on *your* blog! Unless you follow it up instantly with other posts, it's also the first thing many of your first few readers will see.

There are different approaches to writing a first post. Some people like to make a big deal out of it and publish an introduction, while others dive into their niche without even saying hello. Remember, this first post will stay on your blog even after you've published fifty million more, and all your readers, even new ones, will be able to access it via your blog's archives.

Blogger James Chartrand suggests two main ways to write an introductory post: the mission statement, and the essay. The mission statement is short and sweet, summarizing what your blog is about and what you intend to do with it. Even if you do not want to publish your mission statement as a post, write it anyway! It will act as a valuable touchstone for the focus of your blog, reminding you what you set out to accomplish.

Writing an opening essay is more welcoming and personal. It incorporates the content of the mission statement, but goes beyond *what* you want to do and delves into the reasons *why*—to establish who you are, why you're here, and what you're going to do. You can also use it to assure your readers that you know what you're talking about and that you're passionate about your niche. Think back to when you were identifying your niche and your target audience, and establishing your goals. Use what you came up with then as a framework for your introductory essay. Try to answer these questions:

- Why do I want to blog?

- Why do I want other people to see it?

- Why should other people care what I think?

In the earlier stages you were thinking about what your blog means to *you*. Now, broaden your horizons and think about what you want it to mean to other people.

Whether or not you opt to write a welcome post, you should include some information about yourself in a static position somewhere on your blog, accessible to readers if they want to find out more about you. You could include a small bio in the header or sidebar of your layout, or if your theme allows, you can create a dedicated **"About"** page to tell your readers everything you want them to know.

Picking post topics

Carefully consider the topic for each new blog post you write. Choose something current and interesting within your niche. Here's a list of 15 simple techniques to get those creative juices flowing:

1. Mind maps may remind you of school, but they're a useful tool and should never be forgotten. Write down everything you can think of about your niche that is currently popular. Was a new product just announced or released? Did a prominent figure do something noteworthy? Are there any important events coming up?

2. Find a question that needs answering. Check sites like Yahoo! Answers and Ask.com to find questions that people are asking. You can also use the predictive feature of search engines: type in a question word like what, who, or why _____, and watch what appears in the drop-down list! (Warning: some of these may be pretty strange...)

3. Use Google Alerts. Remember your keyword research? Use keywords to set up a series of alerts for topics in your niche. Every day, Google will deliver a bunch of ideas straight to your inbox, hot off the press. Don't delete these alerts even if you do not use them straightaway, as you may want to revisit them later.

4. Keep track of the news by reading newspapers, watching TV, and visiting news sites. You need to be ahead of the game when it comes to your niche. If your niche is particularly specialized and rarely features news, consider subscribing to a specialist publication.

5. Don't just aim to stay ahead of the curve; *think* ahead of it, too. Think about the direction your niche is taking. Don't be afraid to speculate! For example, when the iPhone 4S was released, tech blogs have published speculative articles about the next model. Each time a new bit of information about the iPhone 5 was released or leaked, it acted as a springboard for another set of predictions. Of course, when the phone was finally released these blogs also posted reviews. You can do the

same; compare the reality of what happens to your own and/or others' predictions, seeing what you all got right or wrong.

6. Remember those competing blogs you studied for research? Keep going back to check on what they're posting. Consider whether you have an interesting take on the same material. You can even write a direct response to someone else's post, agreeing, disagreeing, or adding to what was said. You can then link back to the original post, beginning a mutually beneficial relationship with the other blogger, who may throw some links your way in the future.

7. Don't always play it safe. Safe writing is often boring. Controversial topics receive a lot of attention, especially when the writer challenges a dominant opinion. When entering into this territory, however, be sure to put your argument forward reasonably. But remember, not all battles are worth the offense, and the subsequent fallout you could cause.

8. Join a blogging group or community. Here you can share ideas with like-minded bloggers and build relationships that will help you build up your presence in the blogosphere (see Part Six).

9. Consider using interviews. Interviews can produce interesting posts. For a comprehensive guide on how to interview absolutely anyone, check out this article.

10. Ask your readers what they want. You can do this through a blog post, or you could target your most active commenters through e-mail. They'll be flattered you chose them. You can also use polls, Tweets, and Facebook status updates to mine your readers' wishes and opinions. You'll likely be surprised by the number of eager suggestions you receive! Be sure to credit the source of your inspiration if you do write a post on a topic suggested by a reader. Saying "thanks" costs nothing and it'll enhance your relationship with your readers by demonstrating that you appreciate their contributions.

11. Comments—both positive and negative—are a valuable source of ideas. Again, be sure to credit the source if you use a commenter's idea.

You can even be sneaky and review the comments on a competing blog, see what your competitor's readers want, and then give it to them first!

12. Reviews make great material and are always in demand. You can review absolutely anything related to your niche: the latest products, books, or films. This paves the way for advertising and affiliate opportunities (covered in Part Seven).

13. Check to see what's buzzing on social media and networking sites. Keep an eye on which stories and videos are trending on Facebook and Twitter. Twitter hashtags are a great way to identify current hot topics. Hashtags.org is a Twitter # directory with a simple, user-friendly interface. It shows the performance of each topic, including the number of times it's mentioned each day.

14. Create an aggregate post. This is a post where you pull together many interesting links about a particular topic, creating a valuable resource. For example, Fuel Your Blogging publishes regular posts titled "The Hot List of Links for Bloggers," while the Drudge Report is a site fueled entirely by aggregate content, with no original posts. Compiling a useful list of links for your readers shows that you are able to recognize quality content other than your own. Don't just post the links themselves: be sure to summarize, use excerpts, and provide comments to show that you've explored the site and evaluated its use.

15. Invite another blogger to write a guest post. This gives you a bit of a break and builds your relationship with another blogger at the same time. Beware of becoming dependent on guest posts, though. We'll talk more about guest posting in Part Six.

If you have an idea that seems too big for one post, consider breaking it down into a series. This can keep readers coming back to your blog, knowing the next entry in a series is due each Monday, for example. After the series is complete, you could even turn it into an e-book that you can distribute to your readers, for free or for a profit.

The best way to make sure your blog will be read is to create readers who need to read you. A great way to do this is to be a problem solver. For example, if your blog is about home remedies, you are giving your readers something they need—cures for their afflictions. Your topics can also address more general or less practical needs, such as the need to be entertained (possibly the trickiest of all to fulfill!).

A great way to ensure that your posts are tailored toward your readers' needs is to remember the acronym GDP. This stands for:

Goals, Desires, Problems

Everyone has **goals** they want to achieve, **desires** they wish to fulfill, and **problems** that need to be solved. If you can appeal to one or two of these issues (three is a push in one post), you'll end up with a blog your audience cannot afford to miss.

Popular post templates

Even when you are clear about your topic, it can be difficult to communicate your information in a way that readers will enjoy reading. Good formatting is a big help in getting clear messages and information across. Here are some basic descriptions and examples of popular blog post formats:

- **List posts:** A list post can be a list of absolutely anything. Aggregate posts consist of a list of links. Also popular is the "list of reasons" post: why you should invest in high-quality hair straighteners; why Harry Potter is the best wizard ever; why blue is a good color for bedrooms. You can write about literally anything in this simple format. The number of items is usually cited in the post title. The humor site Cracked.com publishes many list posts on topics ranging from movies to health, with several unique titles.

- **"How to" posts:** This is a surefire winner if you pick something that people want and need to know how to do. It directly addresses an issue that, by the end of the post, will be resolved (if you write clear instructions, that is). eHow.com is a web site dedicated to "how to" articles that address all aspects of life.

- **Narrative posts:** Narrative posts are common on personal blogs. They tell a story, often beginning with sentences like "The other day I..." or "Something happened last week...." They can tell a story about something that has happened or is happening to you, or you can share a story told to you by a friend, or even something overheard in the grocery store. Narrative posts can be a little trickier to sell, as the benefit to the reader isn't immediately obvious. The benefit may be that the story is cathartic in some way, generating laughter or tears, or perhaps the story reveals a moral or life lesson. The important thing in a narrative post is to keep your readers "hooked." Make them care what happens next, and keen to know how the story ends.

- **Micro blogging:** Micro blogging is a relatively new phenomenon, encouraged by the hosted blogging platform Tumblr. Micro blogging straddles the gap between the blogosphere and Twitter. As a result, these posts are very concise, often just a couple of sentences long. The post could be a joke, or a phrase. The Clients from Hell Tumblr is regularly updated with short, amusing accounts of exchanges between designers and their clients, for example, when a client insisted an image wasn't square.

- **Reviews:** Blog posts that review products or services. The best way to approach a review is to break the subject down into various features, and review each one individually before bringing your findings together in a summative conclusion. In a smartphone review, for example, you would probably talk about the aesthetic features of the device, the operating system, its processor and memory capacity, and its camera separately, before evaluating its success. Shawn Blanc posts a lot of detailed technology and gadget reviews on his blog. For example, see his in-depth exploration of changes, updates, and nitpicks found in Mac OS X 10.8.

- **Debate posts:** These are usually served best when you have a strong argument as the basis of your topic. Here, each section or paragraph presents a new stage in your argument. You can also address and potentially rebut counter-arguments to strengthen your position. A debate post doesn't have to come to a decisive conclusion one way or the other; it can express both or several sides of an issue. The Opinionator blog from the *New York Times* discusses issues like politics and economics, including controversial topics like the morality of migration, by offering a broad range of perspectives.

Unless your blog will be dedicated to one type of post (for example, a "how to" blog, like eHow), it's good to try and mix up the kinds of posts you publish.

Crafting a headline

The headline of a blog post is its title. Displayed at the top of the post itself, it's also what appears on Twitter, Facebook, RSS feeds, in your blog's archives, and in search engine results. Your headline is the bait you use to hook all the browsers, skimmers, and surfers out there before reeling them in to the main body of your post, where your blog's content can convert them into regular readers. The primary purpose of your headline, as Brian Clark points out, is to get the first line of your post read. If it can't do that one essential job, all the time and effort you put into the post as a whole will be wasted.

There is a legendary 50/50 rule, which suggests that half the time you spend on the post should be spent *entirely* on writing the title. Similarly touted is the 80/20 statistic, which states that although 8 out of 10 people may read your headline, only 2 out of 10 will read the actual post. Fortunately, there are plenty of tips and tricks to help you craft an interesting and magnetic headline.

First, you must accept that people are a pretty selfish bunch—always asking, "But what's in it for *me*?" Your headline needs to answer that question before your readers have time to ask it. You must promise to give them something they need. It could be a product, celebrity gossip, or a recipe for pumpkin pie. Your headline makes the promise that your content then fulfills, or else readers will quickly learn that your promises aren't worth much.

Here are some basic tips to bear in mind when crafting headlines:

- **Keep it (reasonably) short:** Although your headline can be long if it needs to be, snappy headlines grab readers' attention before they get a chance to get bored. SEOmoz recommends that you aim at keeping your headlines below 70 characters: this is the maximum limit Google displays in search results.

- **Make your offer believable:** If you claim that you know how to make readers a million dollars overnight, undoubtedly some people will click through, wanting it to be true—but they'll quickly leave once they realize it's an offer you cannot fulfill. You want readers to feel confidence in your promise. *Instead*, be specific about what you *can* do: "I can help you save $100 in less than 5 days" is far more likely to be true.

- **Make the headline directly relevant to the content:** Readers do not want to access your post expecting one thing and then end up getting another. They will find it equally off-putting if you divert them with extraneous, irrelevant information beyond the scope of the headline. They'll feel you've tricked them and they'll leave with no plan to return.

In *The Copywriter's Handbook,* Bob Bly identifies eight different types of headlines. Run through this list and see if one of these templates helps you produce an appropriate title for your post:

- **Direct:** This headline gets straight to the point, doesn't use clever wordplay, and is totally literal.

- **Indirect:** Indirect headlines are more subtle, often playing on words with double meanings, or creating witty combinations that evoke curiosity in the reader.

- **News:** News headlines are similar to direct headlines, getting straight to the point. They announce the news value of the post outright.

- **How to:** This headline must communicate the benefit the article offers its readers.

- **Question:** These headlines ask a question readers can empathize with or want answered.

- **Command:** A command headline is direct and assertive, usually beginning with a strong verb calling the audience to action.

- **Reasons why:** This headline follows the format of "x reasons why" and can be used to introduce list posts. For example, "8 Reasons Why Headlines Are Important."

- **Testimonial:** A testimonial headline uses a quote from an authoritative figure or celebrity relevant to your niche, using big names to draw people in and add credibility to your claims.

As important as crafting a compelling, well-written headline is, the appearance of keywords in the headline can also be relied on to draw in readers. The careful placement of one or two keywords, in an appropriate context, will help search engines direct readers to your post. As always, it's a case of trying to optimize traffic without becoming a slave to SEO.

Creating an outline

Most people groan at the thought of writing an outline, but it really doesn't have to be a complicated, lengthy process to be effective, especially where blogging is concerned.

Simplify the process; think of "outlining" as a plan of action, rather than a detailed description of the path your blog will take.

In this guide, we've discussed headlines first, but you don't have to formulate all posts in this order. You may prefer to write the outline first, followed by the headline and content. Alternatively, you may find it easier to leave the headline until last.

Sit down with your headline and ask yourself what points need to be addressed in order to fulfill the offer it makes. Write them down, and determine how they can be arranged so that your content progresses fluidly from one point to the next. It's as simple as that.

Subheadings can help to organize content so that it flows smoothly. Even if you do not plan to use subheadings in the finished post, they can still be useful in the planning stage to establish the focus of each paragraph. Each section should address a new feature, point, or development of your argument. You want your readers to feel like they are progressing with you through your post, rather than standing still.

Consider each section and ask yourself:

- Does this point add to my argument?

- Does this point provide the reader with new information?

- Have I already covered this point elsewhere?

If you cannot determine the purpose of a paragraph within your post, it probably doesn't need to be there. If readers begin to read whole sections that have no identifiable purpose, they will feel lost or misdirected and move on. Keep them hooked by presenting information in a logical, progressive order. If a point needs to emerge twice, or two similar points need to be made in the same post, vary your language so it doesn't appear repetitive.

Content is king

This is the cardinal rule of content writing. Although keywords and SEO may generate traffic, no one wants to read bad writing. Readers want something engaging and interesting that directly addresses and fulfills a need. Content may be king, but only good content will make a great king.

Another acronym of writing wisdom passed around the web is AIDA, which stands for:

Attention, Interest, Desire, Action
Let's break it down:

- Your headline grabs the audience's attention.

- The first few sentences or first paragraph stimulates their interest, getting them to read on.

- Your content directly appeals to a desire they have, whether it's to lose weight, buy a car, or even just the desire to laugh.

- By the end, the post has convinced them to act. This could be buying the product you're selling, clicking an affiliate link, or subscribing to your blog so they can enjoy reading your posts in the future.

Remember, your blog posts are a conversation between you and your readers. The last paragraph of your post is almost as important as the first. The last paragraph should leave a positive impression of you that will convince them to return.

Furthermore, make sure that you reach a satisfying conclusion. It's bad form to end your post by leaving readers hanging without a summary or goodbye.

The exception, though, is if you leave your post open-ended on purpose to stimulate discussion. Here are a few examples of post topics and appropriate exit questions:

- **A post about the writer's fear of sharks:** "What's your biggest fear?"

- **A post about a sacrifice the writer made to make his or her partner happy:** "What's the biggest thing you've ever given up for a partner?"

- **A post about a new necklace the writer bought, which is now his or her favorite piece of jewelry:** "What's your favorite piece of jewelry, and why?"

Note how each of these questions is directly related to the post topic, but extends the issue directly out to the reader. If you do use an exit question like this, be sure to respond to the reader comments. The issue you addressed can lead to an interesting, ongoing conversation.

Writing tips and techniques

There's a popular quote among writers: "Easy reading is damned hard writing." Simple writing is a paradox: it's the easiest to understand, but often the most difficult to produce.

People do not want to waste time and energy deciphering one post out of the millions published every day. If they do not get the gist quickly, they'll lose interest, and you'll lose a reader. Keep reminding them of what's in it for them, and stay focused. If you go off-topic, you will stray into territory your readers do not care about, and they'll be gone.

In this section, we'll cover some basic areas of writing, language, and layout that will help you to communicate your message and keep your readers hooked.

Sentences, structure, and spacing

The easiest way to keep your writing simple and fast-paced is to use short, digestible sentences. Complicated, difficult-to-read sentences are not necessarily better writing. When using longer sentences, make sure the meaning is clear and that they are framed by short sentences to maintain the pace. If you're aiming for a narrative style post, try using longer sentences for slower moments and shorter sentences for dramatic ones. Avoid paragraphs of long sentences, since that kind of wall of words will cause the casual reader to leave your blog quickly without reading *anything*.

Adding space between paragraphs and leaving areas of the screen blank is called adding whitespace. Interspersing your posts with a reasonable amount of whitespace makes them easier on the eye. There are other techniques you can use to break up the page.

Bullet points and numbered lists may seem clichéd and overused, but there's a reason for that: they work! Lists break information down into digestible chunks. Moreover, lists can:

- Draw attention

- Make information more concise and easier to understand

- Communicate whole points quickly and effectively

Here are a few other ways to break up text and create whitespace:

- Images such as photographs, clipart, and drawings

- Charts and graphs

- Small text boxes featuring brief information, like quotes or statistics

You need to convince your readers they're going to get something out of your post; something worth more than the time and effort they put in to read it. In addition, if your posts have great value for your readers, they'll be more likely to want to share them with others.

Specificity and credibility

Specificity is an essential part of blog writing. Research is important, because readers will sense if you haven't put in the work. Statistics, references, and testimonials will help convince readers that you're a reliable source of information and encourage them to keep coming back for more.

Specificity is also enhanced by giving examples. Your description of an event or emotional experience should be specific enough for the reader to picture it vividly in his or her mind. This deepens the reader's engagement with your content. Try appealing to multiple senses by describing sounds and smells, as well as sights.

Though being specific is important, remember not to bore your readers to death with an account of every word played in your last game of Scrabble. Details should enhance your posts, not drag them down.

Making an offer

The purpose of your blog is to get readers to buy what you're "selling." It may be a product, service, idea, or opinion. With each post, you are making an offer. The headline is an invitation, while the rest of your content convinces readers to take you up on that offer. By the end of each post, you should have established what the offer is, and convinced the reader it's worth their time (and, in some cases, money) to take you up on it. You can do this by stressing the benefit they will receive. If you do this successfully you'll get what you want, be it a sale, subscription, or positive comment on the post.

If you feel your posts aren't persuasive enough to make the sale, try going back to the outline stage and re-examining your points. Think about each one, and try to identify the benefit to the reader. If you cannot think of any benefits, that particular point may not be a compelling part of your argument and it could probably be removed. You need to convince the reader that what you're selling is something they need.

Be assertive

Be bold and firm when making your offer, and stand behind what you say, even if it's controversial. This is an important aspect of responding to reader feedback as well. However, be careful to recognize when confidence and assertiveness may be turning into arrogance. This can have the opposite effect, alienating your audience rather than convincing them of your authority.

Another top tip for being assertive is to avoid the passive voice.

The passive voice is boring and gloomy. You need your writing to be zippy and fast-paced. If you think you might be using the passive voice, look for "being" verbs, like is, are, was, were, and been. So instead of:

"The bone was chewed by the dog." Use the active voice, and say: "The dog chewed the bone."

To stay in the active voice, make sure you start sentences with the subject—the noun that *does* something. In the passive voice, sentences often start with the object—the noun that has something *done* to it. So in our example, the subject of the sentence is "the dog" (active voice), while the object of the sentence is "the bone" (passive voice). Remember this simple rule and try keeping your blog posts in the active voice. An added benefit of the active voice is that it helps keep posts concise. Writing in the passive voice often uses a lot of unnecessary words.

Repetition and comparisons

Repetition isn't always a bad thing. When used well, repetition can be a powerful persuasive device. Start by stating the point directly, and then reinforce it with an example from a story or anecdote. Use an analogy to make the point clearer. Back it up with a quote from a notable figure. At the end of the post, summarize the point concisely to make sure your readers have really gotten the message.

Using techniques like metaphors, similes, and analogies can help reiterate important points in interesting ways. Analogies in particular are great ways of breaking down complicated information in a way readers can easily understand. Writing coaches will always advise you to show, not tell. Using these techniques, you engage your readers' imaginations in a way that involves them in the experience you are describing.

Focusing on the reader

The readers are the most important focus of your posts—make them feel special, as if you are singling them out and talking directly to them. Do this by shifting the focus toward your target audience, and away from you. Maximize "you" and minimize "I" and "me."

But, what if your blog is very personal and you often write about yourself and your experiences? What if you like to feature anecdotes and stories in the first person? There is room for "I" and "me" in such blog posts, and often it is the personal element of blog writing that draws people in, making them feel that they are conversing with a real person.

A great way to make sure that the focus of your posts swings back to the reader is to use the exit question technique we mentioned earlier. Don't be afraid to ask your readers what they think and how they feel. You can also ask questions throughout your posts, stimulating your readers' minds as they think about the answers.

Getting personal

If you want your posts to be passionate and compelling, you need to inject them with some emotion. To do this, be honest about your feelings; open up to your reader. Don't be afraid to show them who you are and why you're here. Sure, some people might make a few negative comments, but most will admire you for your bravery. They will be able to relate to you far more easily if they can see who you are.

Empathy is an important trait in a blogger, especially when you consider that you're trying to appeal to readers' needs. Presenting a solution is a good thing, but demonstrating that you understand the problem is even better. Instead of just throwing your idea or product straight out there, identify why your readers need it. Think of it as a process of agitate and solve.

Your presence should be a tangible element of your blog and its posts. Readers should be able to identify your voice in everything you write and learn to distinguish it from the voices of other bloggers. Having a distinctive voice will also make you a memorable guest blogger. Don't be afraid to tell your own stories and use examples from your life, and you will often find readers falling over their feet to tell you their own anecdotes in return. You're aiming for what Margaret Andrews calls the OMGMT response—posts that make your readers say, "Oh my God, me too!"

A major part of establishing your blogging voice is expressing your opinions. Opinions are what separate blog posts from, say, the news. People read blogs for perspective, not objectivity. Don't be afraid to give your opinion and ask for other people to share theirs. People enjoy finding out what other people are thinking, so opinions are engaging. Share them, and your readers will feel like they're getting to know you.

If you feel strongly about something, say so.

Being brave enough to fight in your corner isn't the only way to show courage in your blogging. Exhibit self-awareness by admitting your flaws; your readers will love you for it. If you make a genuine mistake, do not cover it up. It shows that you are human and humble. Sincerity will win the hearts of your readers, while artificiality will push them away.

Length of posts

The proper length of a blog post is often debated. Try not to worry about this too much when you are actually writing. It's better to get your thoughts and ideas down on the page while in a creative mindset, without stressing about how long your post will be. You can always cut your posts down later when editing.

Traditionalists insist that blog posts have to be short—no more than 350 words. You may feel you can say everything effectively in that amount of space, but if you have more to contribute, then do not feel constrained. There are bloggers out there who write very long, detailed posts and experience great success. Conversely, there are those who write short posts that aren't so successful. Brevity alone does not impress readers; good writing does.

As a general rule of thumb, though, if you can say it in fewer words, do. Good writers are able to communicate a whole story in a concise post, and blogging is a medium perfectly suited to brevity. Ask yourself:

- Could I break this information down into two posts, or even a series?

- Will my readers care about everything I have said?

- Is the length worth the risk?

A tight argument doesn't need thousands of words to make its point. Get into the habit of cutting words that are extraneous, unnecessary, or superfluous. See? Did that last sentence really need all three of those synonyms? The point could just as easily have been communicated with one. Keep it short and snappy; do not give your readers time to lose interest.

Here are a few examples of common superfluous words and phrases to watch out for in your writing:

- But

- Very

- Just

- Which

- New

- Really

- That

- There are

- In order to

- The fact that

"But," in particular, is often identified as an unnecessary word. The meaning of a sentence is often clear without its presence, and removing it can create tighter text. Go through your latest post and see how many times you used the word "but." Could you have used "and" or a semicolon instead? What about "although," "even though," or "despite"?

Seth Godin is a very successful writer who produces short, pithy blog posts. Because he writes concisely, he's able to get his readers thinking in under 200 words. Although you cannot tackle all sides of an argument in a very short post, you can address different aspects of it in many linked posts so that you get more posts out of each idea.

Brian Clark and the Copyblogger team publish longer posts, usually at least 600 words. In a long post, you can tackle every side of an argument, but you may struggle with the challenge of the task. Depending on your goals, the results may be worth the effort. Statistics show that longer blog posts are more likely to receive reader comments.

The only way to find out which style suits you best is to try them out. Keep practicing until you find what feels like a natural way to handle post length. Write, and write a lot! And then edit!

The importance of editing

James Chartrand recommends that newbie bloggers completely rewrite each blog post not once, not twice, but ten times. Not edit: completely rewrite, from scratch. The idea is that this process helps you better organize your thoughts and improve your style. Each time, the rewrite retains all the best bits of the original, as these are the parts you remember.

Reading through your posts before publishing is a must. There are two factors you need to assess: the content and the writing. We'll start with content, as this is the creatively demanding element.

Read your post. Read it aloud. If you want to, read it to a friend. Think about what you're actually trying to say, and consider what a reader will get out of it. Ask yourself if the post:

- Is relevant to your niche

- Responds to your target audience's needs and interests

- Delivers on the promise made in its headline

Once you've determined whether the content is appropriate and covers all bases, you can switch to the editing mindset. For this process, you need to be as impartial and objective as possible. Because writing and editing require two different mindsets, it's good to leave time between the two processes.

Good editing means you need to disconnect from the content of the post and focus on the quality of the writing. Many writers find it difficult to edit their own material, so if you find yourself in this position, you could ask a friend for help, or outsource your editing to an external agency. Try reading your posts backwards, word by word. This ensures you are entirely disengaged from the content and can focus on other factors like spelling, punctuation, and grammar.

Remember, once you publish something online you can never take it back. Be sure to filter your language and your emotions to produce a post suitable for sharing. One rash post can damage your credibility and reputation. Even if you take a post down immediately, someone probably saw it, and might even have taken a screen shot of it, especially if it was offensive in some way.

Sometimes you may also feel it's necessary to revise a post after it's published. You may realize that some mistakes slipped through the net, or you may receive some feedback from readers suggesting useful alterations you'd like to implement. Interestingly, Tom Chu compares the process of revision to the five stages of grief! Each stage represents an obstacle you must work through:

- **Denial:** Initially, you may see all negative feedback as trolling. At some stage, though, you have to accept that you will write things that some people will not like.

- **Anger:** Avoid getting angry with yourself or with others, especially if they're giving you negative feedback. Don't engage in arguments with commenters. Keep calm and consider their opinions. You may find it useful, even though the truth can hurt.

- **Bargaining:** Don't negotiate with yourself for your content. If something needs cutting, just do it!

- **Depression:** You may sink into self-doubt. "No one will read this anyway! I'm a bad writer!" That's insecurity talking, so push through it.

- **Acceptance:** Finally, you come to accept that editing and revising content is a necessary part of being a writer.

Although editing and revising are essential to becoming a better blogger, you have to recognize when enough is enough. Striving for perfection is great, but not if it inhibits your progress by preventing you from getting anything done. Once posted, do not fret too much over mistakes you may have made. Maybe you'll go back to that post and revise it, maybe you won't. Your readers want good quality content, but they do not expect it to be flawless. After all, your flaws make you human, and therefore relatable, in their eyes.

Pictures and other media

Again, content is king. While you don't want to detract from your writing with loads of pictures and a busy layout, carefully chosen media can add a lot to your blog. Pictures are the main contender, and if you develop techniques to use them effectively, they will complement your content rather than distract from it. Here are a few more reasons you should consider using images in your blog posts:

- According to the Visual Teaching Alliance, around 65% of people are visual learners. The brain processes visual information 60,000 times faster than text.

- Images are able to communicate more information than words due to the preconceived associations people may have with certain images.

- Image processing happens in a different part of the brain than word processing does. By utilizing images, you engage more of your reader's brain.

- An image you include in a post will be displayed when it is shared on sites like Facebook; bold, beautiful images are more likely to be shared.

There are all kinds of different images you can choose to include in your posts. If you're describing an event you took part in, a family pet, or something close to home, you can include a personal photograph. Graphs and charts can be used to back up an argument and explain statistical information. If you're reviewing a product, it's logical to include a product image or two. Literal images are best when representing something specific, while abstract images evoke thoughts and emotions.

You may worry about copyright infringement when adding pictures to your posts. Public domain images are free images you can use without crediting the source or paying a fee. For a comprehensive list of resources, check out the Wikipedia Public Domain Image Resources page. There are also many paid image resource sites where you can purchase higher quality, hard to find images, such as Getty Images and Shutterstock.

To play it totally safe, pick up a camera and shoot your own photos! Many bloggers do this, and some even focus their blogs on the images they capture. If you are looking for very specific images that you cannot create yourself then this isn't an option, and you will need to seek out one of the sources mentioned above.

If you do add an image or two to your blog posts, don't forget the captions! Captions give you a great chance to make a funny or clever comment or elaborate on certain details presented in the image.

Videos

Videos are another good way to add an extra dimension to your blog's content. Embedding videos on your site is now very easy. While you can film your own videos or buy rights as you would for images (both Getty Images and Shutterstock feature videos), many providers will allow you to use their videos' HTML embed codes. These may be displayed beneath the video itself, or when you right click. Look for the words "share" and "embed." YouTube is also a great resource for videos, thanks to its extensive collection of user-uploaded footage.

Both images and videos should be carefully chosen to complement your blog's content and draw your readers deeper into the text, rather than distract them from what's important.

Verifying and crediting sources

Although a blog isn't a news article or an academic essay, verifying and crediting sources is important if you want to build a reputation as a trustworthy source. If you do not use reliable sources, you risk your reputation, and you're also contributing to the perpetuation of false information. Potentially, this could lead to the defamation of a person or organization, which could get you into a lot of trouble.

When considering an article or blog as a potential source, do not assume that the information you are reading is fact. Luckily, most articles and blogs cite their sources well, so you can dig deep into the roots of the information to check the validity of a source.

Also, remember to always link back to your sources. You can either have a list of sources at the end of your post, or incorporate your references within the text. This way, readers have the option of exploring the issue further by seeing where you got your information. It's also a great way to build relationships with other blogs, as you're giving them "link-love" by sharing your traffic with them.

PART FIVE: A BLOG IS FOR LIFE

The update debate

How often you should update your blog has become a bit of a controversial topic. Some bloggers have a schedule they stick to; it might be every Wednesday, Tuesday, and Friday, or even every day at the same time. Others are more casual, writing a post whenever they feel inspired. There are good and bad elements to each approach.

Consistency is important for building a solid readership base. If readers know exactly when you post, they will know that when they come back they will not be disappointed. When a new reader stumbles across your blog, they're more likely to stick around if the last post was fairly recent. If a blog looks like it's been abandoned, readers will abandon it, too.

That doesn't mean that you have to force yourself to publish a post every day. Forcing yourself to write content will probably result in poor, dispassionate writing. If you have something post-worthy every day, go right ahead and post. But do not feel like you have to! A weekly schedule of one or two posts a week is perfectly acceptable.

Moreover, many writers and writing coaches suggest setting yourself a daily writing quota. Start with 100 words per day and work up. You could write in a journal, compose a letter, or do a creative writing exercise. Just make sure that your writing muscles are getting regular exercise so that they get stronger! Try to write a quota of words rather than writing for a time period. Words are words, while two hours could produce zero words if you sit there twiddling your thumbs.

Handling blogger's block

Bloggers are writers, and that means they're at risk for developing the debilitating condition known as writer's block. Have you ever heard the phrase "an ounce of prevention is worth a pound of cure"? The best way to avoid writer's block is to write, every day.

If you consider your blog to be a job, treat it that way. Get professional. Would you decide not to go to work just because you knew it would be a difficult day? No! You'd get on with it, or risk losing your job. Treat writing the same way. Some writers, like blogger Beth Hayden, have a writing "uniform." In Beth's case, this is nothing fancy, just sweats. Putting on the sweats puts her in a productive mindset that says, "Now is the time to write."

Another good way to stave off blogger's block is to keep reminding yourself *why* you blog. Never forget those goals you wrote down way back in Part One. If it helps, consider sticking notes or pictures above your desk that help you visualize your goals while you work. Remember that you aren't being forced to blog; you're in control, and this is your enterprise. Through your blog, you're providing people with something they need. If you remember that your blog posts will enrich other people's lives, you may find it easier to push on.

If a project is really looming overhead and you just can't face it, try breaking your project down into smaller chunks. If it's a singular blog post, work on each section one by one (and not necessarily in chronological order). If you're working on a series of posts, careful planning of each post will help you stay focused. Keep all of your planning materials, as these will help remind you that you're working toward an achievable goal.

What if nothing works and you're just stuck in a creative rut? There may be an underlying issue inhibiting your writing. Creativity stems from the mind, body, and soul. Stress is a major factor behind writer's block, whether at work, home, or in another area of your life. Taking care of yourself and making sure you're healthy and relaxed is a good way to conquer a creative slump.

Jennifer Blanchard recommends a week long "Creativity Cleanse" for severe cases of blogger's block. Here are a few of her tips:

- **Go tech free for a day:** take a break from the gadgets and gizmos that now govern our everyday lives

- **Read something good:** pick something you really *want* to read, whether it is classic literature or a best-selling thriller

- **Eat healthily and drink water:** healthy body, healthy mind

- **Keep active and exercise:** get those creative juices flowing again

- **Try meditating:** even just a short meditation each day

- **Get enough sleep:** lack of sleep can cause problems, including struggling with tasks you usually enjoy

Creating a writing schedule

Writing schedules aren't suited to everyone. Some people work best without a framework, while others find that a schedule increases productivity. It's up to you to decide which method is right for you. Some writers prefer to dedicate a whole afternoon or day to producing a large amount of content. They may do this once or twice a week. Other writers choose to write at the same time, and for the same amount of time every day. They may produce a smaller amount of content on a more consistent basis.

The most important thing is to figure out when you're at your productive and creative peak. This is when you'll produce your best material. Don't force yourself to adhere to anyone else's patterns; if you're not a morning person, work in the evening. If you're feeling strained and under pressure, it'll show in your work. Ideally, you should schedule writing for a time when:

- You're free from other responsibilities and will not be distracted

- You enjoy writing

- You're at your most productive and creative

Managing your posts is another consideration when planning your writing time as a blogger. Blogging is not always as simple as writing and immediately publishing. Planning ahead allows you to factor in time for editing, and to schedule "live" posts days, weeks, and even months in advance. Blogger Brandon Cox separates blogging into two approaches: blogging as you go, which means you write posts when inspiration strikes and publish them shortly afterwards, and blogging ahead, where you plan and write your posts ahead of time.

Blogging as you go allows you to:

- Cover real time stories and breaking news

- Be more passionate in your posts, because you're writing about what's currently on your mind

- Show your readers you are present and active on the web

The downsides are:

- Constant stress of thinking up new material on the spot

- Disappointing your readers when you take time off

- Shorter posts that are more reactive than active

Blogging ahead allows you to:

- Structure your content over time, balancing your subject with the kinds of posts produced

- Plan a series of interlinked posts

- Relieve the stress of immediate deadlines

- Blog consistently

- Promote material before it's published

But, this can also lead to:

- A lack of constant pressure, so you become complacent and produce mediocre content

- Missing out on real-time events and breaking news

- Becoming predictable

As with any new hobby or job, you may have to practice for a while before you find the blogging schedule that best reflects your most creative self.

Reader interaction

Once you've had your say in a post, it's the readers' turn. Most blog platforms include a comments section where readers can comment, interact with you, and exchange thoughts with other readers. While the option to turn comments off exists, most successful bloggers advise against this.

Shawn Blanc writes, "Blog comments are like cash: they make a horrible master, but a wonderful slave." Many bloggers feel that enabling comments is essential. It shows that you're open to reader response and even criticism.

Blanc has disabled comments on his blog and suggests that doing so relieves the pressure on readers to feel they *have* to respond. Instead, he encourages readers with genuine feedback to contact him directly via e-mail, Twitter, or instant messaging. While this may be effective in special cases, or with well-established blogs, in general, readers will expect you to provide an easy way for them to comment. In the early stages of your blog, when you are developing your community, we recommend enabling comments.

Be careful when moderating comments. You will need to devote time and energy to moderating comments in order to eliminate spam and trolls, or allow them to appear and risk losing readers as a result. However, not all negative responses should be ignored. If a reader's opinion is expressed thoughtfully and politely, there's no justification for removing it.

Aside from showing that you are open to other perspectives, these kinds of comments often promote discussion beyond the boundaries of the original post. Readers may debate with one another, as well as with you. Constructive criticism and observations can help you grow, and your readers will appreciate your willingness to participate in this process. Allowing people to disagree with you has its benefits. Make a special effort to respond to readers who ask questions, either by commenting back or writing a post. After announcing he'd be blogging full time, Shawn Blanc received e-mails asking him how it was going. In response, he wrote a detailed blog post. You could even pull numerous reader questions together in a FAQ-style post.

Make an effort to respond to your readers in other ways, too. Reply to e-mails, even if it's just to say that you're too busy to respond in detail but you appreciate them getting in touch. To prevent readers from feeling ignored if you're often too busy to reply, consider adding a disclaimer to your blog, warning readers that although you appreciate their feedback you will not be able to e-mail back every time.

Some blogs require logins and account creation before you can comment, which can be off-putting unless the blog is well established. Also, your comments section should be directly below each post, not buried underneath ads, social links, and other distractions.

Most importantly, be accessible. Let people know they can contact you. Make your contact details easily available. Some platforms will even let you create a dedicated contact page, where you can list your e-mail address, instant messaging ID, and Twitter and Facebook addresses, plus anything else you can think of. Be wary of giving out personal details like your home address and phone number, though. Safety first!

Tracking your progress

Tracking your progress is a great way to stay motivated as you expand your blog. You can use tools like Google Analytics to assess your blog's stats, such as how much traffic you receive and the average length of time a reader spends on your blog. Remember though, it's not numbers you're trying to build up—it's readers!

PART SIX: GETTING IT READ

Utilizing search engine optimization

Taking steps to ensure your blog arrives at the top of search results is known as SEO. Many people find SEO intimidating, and associate it only with keyword research. There's much more to SEO than that!

When people search for keywords in your niche, you want them to find your blog at the top of the page. Searchers are more likely to click on links at the top of the first page of results: the links further down and on subsequent pages receive less attention.

Rank highly in search engines like Bing, Yahoo, and Google, and you will have a successful, well-read blog. To achieve this, you must jump through certain hoops to make your blog more appealing to the search engine's page ranking systems. Your site will be ranked alongside others according to how useful the search engine thinks it is. Blogs that appear trustworthy and reliable are considered more likely to produce useful content. Here are a few tips to promote the useful content quotient of your site:

- Verify and credit sources

- Establish back-links from other sites

- Don't fill your blog with links and ads, search engines read link-laden sites as spam

Search engines will consider your blog as a whole, as well as individual pages when ranking. "Unhelpful" content will bring down the rankings of your other posts, which can cost you the top spot in the search results. The more useful posts there are on your blog, the higher the page ranking. Therefore, it's wise to assess your content.

Last year, Google's Webmaster Central Blog posted a list of questions providing guidance on how Google assesses web page quality. You can view the full list online, but here's a selection:

- Would you trust the information presented in this article?

- Does the site have duplicate articles on the same or similar topics with just slight keyword variations?

- Would you recognize this site as an authoritative source when mentioned by name?

- Is this a page you'd want to bookmark, share with a friend, or recommend?

- Would users complain when they see pages from this site?

Take a step back from your blog and ask yourself these questions. While a new blog may not yet be an authority on anything, if you present accurate information in an accessible format, there's no reason why it cannot become one. Getting search engines on your side will really help to boost your readership.

Don't forget keywords, though. Page rankings are determined by complex algorithms, but the main factors are keywords and the amount of traffic the page already receives. It will take time for your blog to climb up the rankings for broad keywords like "movies," but you can use long-tail keywords as a starting point. These are more specific search terms, like "Golden Age Hollywood movies." Searches using long-tail keywords are looking for something specific, so give it to them. You'll gain traffic and your site will gradually rise up in the rankings for broader keywords as well.

Readers vs. traffic

Whether from subscribers, Twitter followers, or "Likes" on Facebook, any increase in attention may seem great at first. However, there's a difference between numbers and readers. SEO, keywords, and back-links are designed to generate raw traffic, which consists of browsers and scanners. Without compelling content, the traffic won't stop long enough to read, subscribe to, or comment on your writing.

Getting visitors to subscribe to your blog via RSS feed or e-mail is the first step in building up a core readership. This way, readers will be alerted every time you post. Seeing your blog and post titles pop-up in their inbox may be the reminder they need in order to keep reading. Visitors exploring your site for the first time may fully intend to come back to your blog, but it's a busy world and they could easily just forget. Make sure subscribing is easy by placing your "subscribe" or "sign up" buttons in a prominent location, such as the top of the page.

RSS feeds are convenient, but not everyone uses them. If you want to send information to readers the old-fashioned way, you need a mailing list. You can use tools like AWeber and Mail Chimp to build e-mail lists. These tools compile and maintain lists when readers enter an address into a bar you embed on your blog. You can create dynamic mail-outs using design templates, or set up auto-responders to send messages at set times.

Willy Franzen details the great results he achieved when he changed the words used to ask readers to sign up on his blog. He realized that to many people the word "subscribe" still has connotations of a paid service, like magazine subscriptions. When he changed "subscribe" to "get," his subscription rate increased by 254% in 8 days.

One of the best ways to encourage readers to connect with you is to explain how they can easily do it in your blog. If you're trying to build Twitter followers, for example, write a post about it! Tell them exactly where the links are on your page or type out your Twitter name so they can easily add you.

Speaking of Twitter, consider following a few of your readers back. This can be useful in the early stages of your blog when you're building up your first few subscribers. Your readers will feel like you have a friendly connection extending beyond the blog.

Taking an interest in your readers' blogs will have a similarly positive effect. It's also possible you will find guest post slots, guest writers, and inspiration for posts. If you have the time, actively seek out the opinions and valuable feedback of your most loyal readers and frequent commenters.

Social media and sharing

Besides Facebook and Twitter, you can use various sites as springboards for posts, including Digg, Reddit, and StumbleUpon.

When posting links to your blog, don't just copy and paste the URL and hit "publish." Think about the way each site displays your content. Facebook will display an image and the first couple of sentences of the post. While your headline should instantly let readers know what the post is about, a brief, well-worded sentence is a useful complement to this. On Twitter, you need to compress the thrust of each post into less than 140 characters to fit into a single Tweet. Modify your content to suit the venue.

At this stage, the attention you devoted to creating reader-focused content will prove its worth. By now, you have built up some dedicated readers who are the secret weapons in your exposure arsenal. Each time you succeed in creating compelling content for your niche, these readers will want to share it. They, too, will turn to platforms like

Facebook and Twitter, promoting your blog to a wider audience that *you* are unable to reach. Spreading buzz on social media will work, provided you give people something worth talking about.

Rewarding readers

Rewarding your readers helps maintain their loyalty. If you provide them with constant benefits, you keep them hooked. Sonia Simone goes as far as to suggest that you should treat your readers like dogs! The description may sound extreme, but it's true that using positive reinforcement techniques will positively affect your relationship with your readers.

Simone suggests the use of "cookie content" as a form of reward. It could be a secret family recipe you share, or a funny picture of yourself—something that will lighten or improve your readers' day. Mind map anything you think you could produce as cookie content and keep hold of it for when the time comes.

Competitions are another popular incentive. If you're launching an e-book, for example, offer a free copy to the first "x" number of commenters on a specific post. Try contacting your most active readers and offer a reward in return for a testimonial about your blog or a product. You can give them free access to something, offer a discount, or even let them have a product for free if they review it.

Widening your readership base

Developing your blog is a balancing act between appeasing current readers and reaching out to new ones. Always remember your target audience, but keep the new reader in mind as well. If a post references something you mentioned elsewhere, briefly explain it (possibly in parentheses) for newcomers. You do not want them to feel excluded because they do not understand what you mean by "that time with the bear." Even better, link the reference back to the original post. That way, you're encouraging readers to dig into your archives.

Making connections

The blogosphere is a network of communities that are made up of other blogs. This makes the blogosphere a great place for you to network and promote your own material. Just make sure you're respectful when you're on other bloggers' turf.

Remember the blogs you found when researching your niche? Competing sites represent potential readers, guest posts, and friends. Commenting on other blogs (or "comment promotion") is a great way to get your name out there. People will start to recognize you as you repeatedly appear in comments on top blogs within your niche. Soon people will decide that your blog is worth checking out, too.

There's an art to comment promotion, though. If you simply comment on a post with a link to your blog, you're spamming. People will automatically dismiss links like this. Contribute to the discussion before tactfully adding your link, and ensure that the post you link to is relevant to the topic in question. Readers will click through if they think your post expands on or responds to the issue at hand. Give them a reason to visit your blog. Be assertive, but not pushy.

Back-linking is another way to increase blog exposure and an SEO method. Back-links are links from other sites to your blog. These can be links to individual posts or to your whole blog. The more back-links you have, the higher your site will be ranked in search engines. Lots of back-links show that other bloggers and web sites find your site worth sharing. Every link you post in a comment on another blog also creates one more route for readers to discover you. This works both ways; link to other relevant blogs in your own posts. Bloggers will appreciate it and maybe share some "link-love" of their own.

Don't hesitate to contact other bloggers. Let them know you enjoy their work, and direct them to your blog, explaining why they might like it. Convince them that a relationship would be mutually beneficial and make specific suggestions, such as exchanging back-links, comments, or guest posts.

Guest posting

Guest posting is a powerful tool. It can extend the reach of your content, build up your blogger profile, and attract traffic from other blogs. You can write guest posts for other blogs, or invite other bloggers to write for you. Writing a guest post puts you in front of a wider (perhaps entirely new) audience. It also promotes you as an expert in your niche. You'll find that after you start guest posting, your opinion will become more highly valued and your work cited more often. It's like a cameo appearance in a movie. As your reputation builds, you will attract bigger and better blogs who will want to interact with you.

Before proposing a guest post, thoroughly investigate the other blog. Is it within or connected to your niche? Are its readers likely to enjoy your writing? There's no point in writing a guest post on a fishing blog when yours is about fashion. Not all blogs are equal; assess whether guest posting will benefit you and help attract new readers. Show the blog owner you've done your research by linking to other articles on his or her site in the body of your guest post.

Make sure you've read the other blog well, too. To increase your chances of success, approach the blog owner with a fully formed idea for a guest post. It would be awkward if that exact topic had already been covered and you hadn't noticed. Read the comments on the site as well as the posts. See if you can identify something the readers want. When you pitch your idea to the blog owner, show that you recognize the type of posts the site needs. If you're feeling confident, go to the blog owner with a post that is already written. Some blogs will even take content that was previously published elsewhere, especially if it didn't receive much exposure at the time and seems worthy of more attention. Ask the blog owner how much space you'll have to promote yourself. This is usually a couple of sentences at the end of the post, so make them count! Although it's a small space, you can use it to craft the perfect pitch. Try to be witty, and make sure to reference your blog and/or other work. Spark additional interest by mentioning a particularly popular or controversial recent post. Ideally, link readers to your main landing page and a specific post. Include links to Twitter, Facebook, or any other social media sites.

There are different ways to attract guest posters to your own blog. You can contact them directly, or advertise on Facebook or Twitter, or in a blog post. You should also display guest post guidelines, either in a dedicated blog post or, if your platform allows, a static page on your site. Describe what you are looking for in a guest post, including the style of writing, length, whether you expect images, etc. Be careful not to sacrifice your own voice for the luxury of letting guest posters do all the work. This is a quick way to lose your blog's distinctiveness, and subsequently, your readers. MyBlogGuest is an online community where bloggers can connect with other writers in the same niche and arrange guest posts.

PART SEVEN: MONETIZING YOUR BLOG

If your blog is doing well and you've attracted a solid foundation of readers, you're ready to start thinking about making a profit. This is known as monetizing your blog, and there are a variety of ways to go about it.

Patience is key

Patience is important for all bloggers, but even more so if you are hoping your blog will make money or potentially become your primary source of income. You have already put work into building up a base of readers, but you have to be patient and selfless in your dedication to them. You're going to have to give, and give, and give, before they will give something back.

Every purchase opportunity represents a potential risk to the consumer. No one wants to spend money on something they ultimately do not want or cannot use. Consumers are especially wary of Internet sellers, and of the unknown. Low-profile bloggers are much less likely to make a sale than high-profile writers who have proven themselves to be reliable. You have to be willing to invest time and effort in your blog before you see any substantial return. Even after you've made a name for yourself, customers will be cautious. You must maintain a high standard of persuasive prose to convince readers to buy what you're selling.

Marketing your own products

Perhaps you started your blog in order to sell products or services. If this is the case, it's important not to push sales right at the beginning. A blog consisting of post after post about your products is not likely to gain many readers. Instead, you'll need to take the time to write interesting posts related to your products so you can develop a solid audience. Your blog then becomes your personal marketing tool, through which you can promote and sell your product.

You may also find that even though you had no monetization plans at first, at some point you realize there is potential for a profit to be made. You may write an e-book and wish to sell it, or decide that your home cooking blog is the perfect place to start selling your homemade jam. In this case, you should already have an organically built readership base. When you feel you're in a secure position, you can start selling your product.

Remember, if you want readers to act, make it as easy as possible for them to do so. Make sure that the **"Shop"** or **"Buy now"** links are visible, possibly at the top of the sidebar. If you have a post or two dedicated to purchasing your products, give clear, concise instructions. You may direct your customers to an eBay or Etsy shop, or implement a sales system directly on your blog. Consider using an easy-pay e-wallet service like PayPal. A universal and easily accessible method of payment makes it easy for customers to trust your site and say yes to your product.

Affiliates and associates

Many larger retailers and brands run affiliate schemes. You can apply to become an affiliate for Scribendi.com, for example, and then review or recommend products on your blog. To do this, you would include an affiliate link to the product on its site. Each payment made through that link will earn you a small portion of the profit. Be sure to choose products relevant to your niche that your audience will need. If you post links to unrelated products, you won't make any money, and you risk irritating your readers.

If your blog focuses on films or books, relevant affiliate links are obvious. If your blog is in a narrower niche, then you might struggle to think of products to advertise. Keyword research can help. Keyword research tools allow you to look for a specific word and view popular combinations. For example, if your blog is about shoes, you might search for "shoes" and find that there are many hits on the combinations "wedge shoes" and "wedding shoes." You then have two specific products you know people are actively looking for.

Advertising revenue

Advertising is the most common form of blog monetization. There are two main methods of utilizing space on your blog for ads. The first is using a program like Google AdSense, which automatically places ads on your site. You accumulate a payment each time a visitor clicks on an ad. This type of advertising is known as cost-per-click (CPC) or pay-per-click (PPC). You should tailor the ads on your site using appropriate keywords. Your readers will become frustrated and angry if the ads featured on your blog seem irrelevant, taking up space and distracting from your posts. Ads tailored around keywords in high demand will also produce higher CPC.

However, using AdSense won't likely generate enough to rely on blogging as a full-time income. Even if your site gets a lot of traffic, you won't necessarily make money, as visitors may not click on the ads. Although some bloggers do manage to make money from this kind of advertising, it's most effective if your blog caters to a specific need that the advertised product fulfills 100%.

A second method of blog advertising is selling ad space directly to retailers. This requires more work on your part, but you'll secure a reliable monthly payment per ad unit if successful. For example, if you've secured payment for four 125 × 125 ad spaces this month, each priced at $20, you know for sure that you'll receive $80. CPC has nothing like this guarantee. The tricky part is finding advertisers. You could use a third party like BuySellAds, which sells your ad space and takes a percentage of the fee in return.

If you'd like to approach advertisers yourself, make sure your blog is as appealing as possible and construct a persuasive pitch. As always, research is important. Some of the keyword research mentioned in the affiliates and associates section will come in handy. You will need to identify products and people within your niche who would benefit from advertising on your blog, and then convince them to do so.

Statistics can impress potential advertisers, but be careful what you use. Alex Denning advises that your number of RSS feed subscribers is only impressive if it is over 1,000 and rising rapidly, while site visits aren't worth mentioning unless they are over 10,000. If your blog hasn't reached these milestones yet, don't worry. Try using stats to your advantage. For example, mention how the number of RSS subscriptions on your blog increased by 50% in two weeks. Who's to know whether it increased from 10 to 15 or 10,000 to 15,000? You should also cite any flattering testimonials you've received, or if a big blog within your niche has back-linked you. Try creating a mind map of all your blog's selling points, and pick out the strongest of these to form your pitch.

Selling ads yourself means you need to set a price for each ad space. For a young blog, Denning suggests charging around $20 a month for a 125 × 125 sidebar ad. Established blogs with decent followings can get away with $30. You need to use common sense to work out what price range is appropriate, and adjust accordingly as your blog grows. The price advertisers pay for ad space should reflect their potential gain, or they won't be interested. Create a win-win situation where both parties stand to gain.

You can incentivize advertisers to buy ad space for multiple months by offering a discount. Play the numbers to your advantage; try offering a 20% discount when buying two months of ad space instead of one. The standard price of $40 for two months is only reduced by $8, but 20% sounds more impressive.

When selling ads, remember:

- Everyone hates pop-ups. Avoid them at all costs.

- Irrelevant ads will make readers think you're just trying to make money and will damage your credibility.

- Ads seamlessly integrated into your content confuse the reader and can cause them to leave without finishing reading your post.

- Multiple ads plastered everywhere look ridiculous and readers will leave without even bothering with your content.

Ads should be clearly visible, but not annoying, or "in your face." They should be targeted at your audience so that readers will want to click through. With thoughtfully placed, appropriate advertising, your blog will not only be an enjoyable pastime and a way to share your ideas, but also a great source of steady income.

Selling merchandise

Selling merchandise is a form of monetization adopted by very popular blogs. It works particularly well for blogs with iconic logos, art styles, or characters, for example, web comics like xkcd.com. If you feel that you've built up enough of a following to sell merchandise, here are a few examples of products you could create and sell:

- Mugs

- Mouse pads

- Pens

- Posters

- Postcards

Asking for donations

Asking for donations is a monetization technique that works only after you have built up a loyal following. In this case, your readers need to be willing to contribute to the maintenance of your blog. If you want to ask for donations, include information about the means to do so in your blog's sidebar. The best way to accept donations is via an e-wallet service like PayPal. You can also encourage donations through blog posts, but be subtle about it.

The get-rich-quick fallacy

Running a blog for profit is the same as any other for-profit enterprise—essentially, a business. Therefore, you will need to maintain an effective business model if you hope to gain substantial revenue. Be realistic in your goals, and remember that it takes time to build up a readership base loyal enough to even consider buying from you. To enhance your credibility, you may need to spend money to make money by buying a domain name, paying for web hosting, and purchasing keyword research tools. Always remember that your blog is a means to an end and it doesn't automatically provide the end itself. That's up to you.

BONUS: HELPFUL BLOGGING TOOLS AND RESOURCES

Glossary of blogging terms

Throughout this guide, we've used a lot of different terminology to refer to aspects of blog creation and maintenance. There are also many other words you might encounter when exploring the blogosphere. We've included this glossary of blogging terms to help you decipher the meaning of specialist terminology when it comes to everyday words that may have a different meaning or different connotations when used in a blogging context.

Account: Created when you join a web site or community. Membership provides access to exclusive features and tools. Blogging platforms and host providers require you to create an account before utilizing their services.

Activation e-mail: In order to activate an account on a web site, you must often input your e-mail address to receive an activation e-mail. This e-mail often features an activation link that will automatically activate your account and take you to it, or a code that you must use to activate your account manually.

Administration: You are the administrator of your blog. Some sites allow multiple users. Some platforms also feature administration sections where you can manage aspects of your blog account, like settings. Administration tools are visible only to administrative users.

Advertising: Use advertising on your blog to generate revenue, either in dedicated ads or through a blog post. See **external ad** and **internal ad**.

Aesthetic: This term refers to the look and feel of your blog.

Affiliate: Become an affiliate, or enter into a partnership with a brand or company. You can then use affiliate links on your blog, directing readers to products or services to earn a percentage of the profit.

Aggregate: Bringing together separate things to create a whole. Aggregate blogs or blog posts gather a set of related stories or links.

AIDA: A popular marketing formula that stands for Attention, Interest, Desire, Action.

Archive: A list of links to all of a blog's posts, usually displayed in reverse chronological order.

Association: Being aware of cultural and social associations can help you choose appropriate colors, images, and words for your blog posts.

Avatar: A visual representation of a user online; usually a small image displayed beside the user's name, for example, when they comment on a post.

Back-link: Incoming links to a web site or page, i.e., links from an external source. A large number of back-links can increase your search engine ranking, as it suggests a significant number of people find your site useful.

Blog: The word blog comes from the original term "web log," which referred to a virtual journal or diary. Gradually, blogs have developed into one of the most versatile web site formats on the net. A blog usually consists of regular posts, displayed in reverse chronological order.

Blogger: Someone who writes content for one or more blogs.

Blogosphere: The online blogging community, encompassing blogs, bloggers, and readers.

Blog platform: Online resource or downloadable software that allows the creation and maintenance of an online blog.

Body: Can refer to the main area of your blog's web site where posts are displayed. Can also refer to the main section of a blog post, as distinct from the beginning and end.

Bug: A glitch or problem you may encounter with your blogging platform. Bugs should be reported to the platform provider, or, if you're using third-party software, to the developer.

CAPTCHA: A security check consisting of a randomly generated combination of letters and numbers. Ensures that visitors to your site are human, not automated programs.

Check box: You might encounter check boxes when filling in forms on a web site. They can be checked or unchecked, and allow you to opt in or out of certain services, such as newsletter sign-up. They can also be used to indicate consent to a site's terms and conditions.

CMS: Content management system. This is software that allows the user to create and maintain content that can then be hosted online.

Code: References to code in regard to blogging usually mean computer programming languages like HTML or CSS, which are used to build and edit software.

Comment: A textual response, usually brief, to a piece of content.

Community: Generated around a web site, like a blog. Community members interact with one another, using the blog as a focal point.

Connotation: A pre-existing association we have developed with something like a color, image, or word. See **association**.

Compose: The act of writing or creating content.

Content: Material for your blog, potentially consisting of text, images, or other media. Blogs need to be filled with quality content to attract readers.

Control panel: An area that features various tabs and navigation tools to help you explore and maintain your blog.

Core software: Basic software, which can usually be enhanced and developed with additional software and extensions.

Corporate blogger: Corporate bloggers blog on behalf of their company or business.

CPC: Cost-per-click. A term associated with advertising on a blog that refers to the amount of money you receive every time someone clicks on an ad on your site.

Credibility: The reliability of your content.

Crowding: A crowded blog layout means you have too much going on visually, so the blog looks unattractive and is difficult to navigate.

CSS: Cascading Style Sheets. A programming language.

Dashboard: See **control panel**.

Database: A structured set of data. Can be held in a computer and uploaded onto a web server.

Demographic: A particular group or sector of the population.

Design: The look and feel of your blog, encompassing elements like theme and layout.

Developer: Someone who develops software, such as blog plugins or extensions.

Directory: A comprehensive list of links, resources, or other information.

Domain: A space on the web where content can be hosted in web sites, like blogs.

Domain mapping: Having registered a domain name, mapping that domain to a specific blog allows people to find your content when they type in that URL.

Domain name: A string of letters, numbers, and symbols that identify the location of something on the Internet.

Drop-down: A space-saving list or menu, usually identified by a small arrow pointing downwards. Clicking on this arrow, or sometimes hovering over the icon, displays an extended list of options.

Embed: To insert something into a particular space.

Extension: An additional feature, such as a piece of software that can be installed to enhance **core software**.

External ad: An advertisement for an external product or service that may be related to, but not produced by, the site on which it is featured.

Featured: Featured content is given particular attention or prominence. If multiple images are included in a blog post, one of them can be set as the featured image so that it is visible alongside the headline when the rest of the post is not.

Features: Aspects or elements of something. A blog theme may have a variety of different features, for example.

Feed: A continuous stream of information. A blog feed is usually displayed in the body of the blog's front page, and features recent posts in reverse chronological order.

Field: On a form, the areas that ask for information (e.g., username, password, e-mail address, etc.).

Fixed: An element of a blog or page that does not move or change, even if the viewer scrolls down or navigates away.

Footer: The very bottom of the page, sometimes where widgets or ads can be placed.

Forum: A community area where users can interact with one another via various discussion threads using textual messages.

Front page: The main page of a web site. On a blog, this page usually features a blog feed of recent posts in reverse chronological order.

Gadget: Google's Blogger platform's equivalent of a **plugin**.

Gallery: A directory of visual media, such as images or screenshots.

GDP: A popular marketing formula that stands for Goals, Desires, and Problems.

Guest post: A post written by a blogger other than the blog owner or the standard contributor(s).

Hashtag: The hashtag, or #, is used on Twitter to identify a particular topic or idea within a Tweet.

Header: The area at the top of the page, usually displaying the blog title and a tagline, sometimes where widgets or ads can be placed.

Headline: Similar to a newspaper headline, the headline of a blog post is its title.

Hobbyist: A casual blogger who doesn't blog for profit.

Host: A company that provides web hosting on its domain, usually for an annual fee. Many also allow users to purchase and register a **domain name.**

Hosted: A blogging platform that also provides hosting, as opposed to users having to host their blog through a third-party provider.

HTML: HyperText Markup Language—a programming language.

Internal ad: An advertisement for a service or product produced by the same site doing the advertising.

Landing page: The first page a reader sees when visiting a blog.

Keyword: A frequently used word related to a particular topic or niche.

Keyword research: The act of researching the words people are frequently using and searching for.

Layout: The way elements are arranged on a page.

License: Some software requires you to purchase a license before you are able to use it. Often you must renew this license annually, and then you can activate the software itself with a product key.

Link: An object, such as an image or segment of text, which links readers to another web site or a different page of the current site.

Link bait: Any content or feature on a web page that is designed specifically to gain attention and encourage others to link to or share it with others.

Link-love: A casual term to describe when bloggers or Internet users do a favor for their peers, linking readers to their content.

Logo: An image or arrangement of visual features representing a company, brand, or other organization.

Long-tail keyword: A long-tail keyword could more accurately be described as a key phrase. Usually several words that refer to something very specific, rather than the vague associations of a singular keyword.

Mailing list: A list of e-mail addresses to which content, such as newsletters or post alerts, can be dispatched.

Moderation: The act of filtering content contributed to your blog, particularly comments, to remove anything that may be deemed offensive, abusive, or **spam**.

Module: The Typepad and Drupal equivalent of a **plugin**.

Monetization: Taking action that causes your blog to start making a profit.

Navigation: Finding your way around a web site via links to access different pages, aided by tools, such as a navigation bar, which is often displayed across the top of the page just below the **header**.

Newsletter: A regular update on the status of an organization or enterprise.

Niche: A topic. A specific area of interest

Notification: A message or alert to inform you of a change in status, such as new content.

Open source: Software or information that is available free of charge, without requiring a **license**.

Outsource: The act of delegating responsibility to an external source, such as paying a professional service to edit or proofread your writing, or outsourcing the design of your web site to a professional developer.

Page elements: Features present on a page that constitute its design or layout.

Plugin: An extension you can add to your blog to give it extra features.

Pop-up: Something that opens in a new window on your screen. Ads that appear in this way are often dismissed as **spam**.

Post: An individual piece of content on your blog. This could be an article or an image. It can also be used as a verb to refer to the act of publishing content on your blog.

PPC: Pay-per-click. See **CPC**.

Premium: Generally refers to something that is not free and requires payment, for example, WordPress.com's premium themes.

Professional full-timer: A blogger who considers blogging to be a full-time job and the main (and possibly only) source of income.

Professional part-timer: A blogger who considers blogging to be a part-time job, receiving some income from his or her blog.

Profile: A place where people can find information about a user. May include a profile picture.

Profit: Money made from an enterprise after the deduction of expenses.

Pseudonym: A nickname or title that isn't your own. Can be used to conceal your identity and create a new one.

Rich-text: Rich-text format is a way of viewing text simply and easily, without the complications of elements like CSS and HTML. Most blogging platforms offer a basic rich-text editor for producing posts.

RSS: Expanded variously as Rich Site Summary or Really Simple Syndication. A web feed format used to publish frequently updated content, such as blog posts.

Search engine ranking: How highly a site is rated by a search engine, which can affect how high up the site and its pages appear in a list of search results.

Self-hosted: A blogging platform that does not provide hosting, so users must find a third-party provider to host their blog.

SEO: Search engine optimization. Steps one takes to increase the search engine ranking of a site and its pages.

Sharing: The act of reproducing all or part of a piece of content to share with others, often on a dedicated sharing platform, such as Reddit or Pinterest.

Sidebar: An area of your blog that runs down the right-hand side, though it can be on the left, down the center, or absent altogether.

Skin: A term often used as an equivalent for **theme**.

Social media: Media used for social interaction, networking, and sharing of content.

Software: A piece of computer programming that can be used to achieve certain goals or complete certain tasks. May require downloading and installation.

Source: The place from which something, such as information or an image, was obtained.

Spam: Unsolicited communication, distributed indiscriminately and often automated, that is of little use. Spam comments can often be identified by vague remarks and irrelevant links.

Static: See **fixed**.

Statistics: Figures and data that display information.

Subscribe: Sign up for membership, a service, or something similar. Blogs often ask readers to subscribe to their mailing list or RSS feed.

Sub-theme: A subsidiary of a parent theme, created using the Drupal blogging platform.

Swipe file: A tool used by writers. A place to keep resources, ideas, and inspiration for future reference.

Tab: A button or other noticeable marker that holds certain content separate from other content. In an Internet browser, you can have several different web sites open on different tabs. On a blog dashboard or control panel, tabs give you access to different tools.

Tag: A word or phrase used to indicate the content of something, like a blog post or image.

Target audience: The group of people at which your product, service, or blog is specifically aimed.

Template: A base layout for your blog, similar to a **theme**.

Theme: A basic layout and design you can apply to your blog and then customize, at least to a degree.

Third-party: An external individual or organization outside the original party with which you were working.

Timestamp: Information on the date and time of publication that is usually automatically added to a blog post.

Tone: The general feel and attitude of your writing, the equivalent to tone of voice in speech. It can be formal or casual, friendly or cold, passive or aggressive, etc.

Toolbar: A set of tools, often inlinks or tabs, that appear somewhere on the page. Along the top is a common placement, or down the side.

Traffic: The number of visitors to your site, often directed from other locations like search engine results or back-links.

Trending: Topics currently receiving a lot of attention may be considered trending. People are talking about them a lot and sharing content that relates to that topic.

URL: The combination of numbers, letters, and symbols that you type into the URL bar of a web browser to reach a specific area of the Internet, i.e., a web site.

Web server: Web servers store the web sites we access when browsing the Internet.

Widget: Similar to a **plugin**; mini programs that perform an additional function and can be added to your blog to make that function available for readers to use or see.

Word cloud: A visually appealing way to display many different words.

WYSIWYG: What you see is what you get. A way of editing that allows you to create a blog post pretty much as it will appear when published, as opposed to editing code, which looks completely different.

Web sites for bloggers

Although we hope to have covered all the basics in this guide, if you're looking for more information on blogging, there are many other resources out there.

Blogs about blogging

2 Create a Web site: www.2createawebsite.com

Copyblogger: www.copyblogger.com

Bloggerbuster: www.bloggerbuster.com

Daily Blog Tips: www.dailyblogtips.com

Fuel Your Blogging: www.fuelyourblogging.com

How to Make My Blog: www.howtomakemyblog.com

Men with Pens: www.menwithpens.ca

ProBlogger: www.problogger.net

Communities and directories

Blog Engage: www.blogengage.com

BlogFrog: www.theblogfrog.com

Blogging Fusion: www.bloggingfusion.com

MyBlogGuest: www.myblogguest.com

Sharing and social media

Digg: www.digg.com

Facebook: www.facebook.com

Pinterest: www.pinterest.com

Reddit: www.redddit.com

StumbleUpon: www.stumbleupon.com

Twitter: www.twitter.com

Blogging tools

Here's a reminder of the useful blogging tools we've mentioned throughout the course of this guide, plus some extra ideas.

Advertising tools

BuySellAds: www.buysellads.com

Google AdSense: www.google.ca/adsense

Commenting tools

ComLuv: www.comluv.com

Disqus: www.disqus.com

E-wallet tools

Google Wallet: www.wallet.google.com

PayPal: www.paypal.com

Image resources

Getty Images: www.gettyimages.com

Shutterstock: www.shutterstock.com

Wikipedia Public Domain Images Resources:
www.en.wikipedia.org/wiki/Wikipedia:Public_domain_image_resources

Mailing list tools

AWeber: www.aweber.com

Mail Chimp: www.mailchimp.com

Note-taking and dictation tools

Google Docs: www.docs.google.com

Dragon Speech Recognition Software:
www.nuance.com/dragon/index.htm

Evernote: www.evernote.com

SEO and keyword research tools

Google AdWords: www.adwords.google.com

Market Samurai: www.marketsamurai.com

Scribe: www.scribeseo.com

SEOmoz Tools: www.seomoz.org/tools

Statistics and analytics tools

Clicky: www.getclicky.com

Google Analytics: www.google.com/analytics

Woopra: www.woopra.com

Acknowledgments and Works Cited

All references within this text are fully acknowledged and, where possible, linked directly to the source material. We now offer two alphabetical lists of all references and works cited within the body of this guide, excluding the additional links to the material found in the Bonus section. The first list consists of online resources and the second refers to those in print.

Please note that the screenshots were captured using Snagit software from TechSmith.

Online references

About.com

"We Can Do Better": Dr. Seuss on Writing, by Richard Nordquist

http://grammar.about.com/od/advicefromthepros/a/seusswrite09.htm

After6 Services

Movable Type Installation Service

http://after6services.com/services/installation-service/

Movable Type Pro Support

http://after6services.com/support/pro-support/

Amazon

Homepage

http://www.amazon.com/

Ask

Homepage

http://www.ask.com/

AWeber

Homepage

https://www.aweber.com/landing.htm

Bleeding Cool

Homepage

http://www.bleedingcool.com/

Blogger

Homepage

http://www.blogger.com/home?pli=1

Bluehost

Homepage

http://www.bluehost.com/

BuySellAds

Homepage

http://buysellads.com/

Clients from Hell

Homepage

http://clientsfromhell.net/

Hip to be Square

http://clientsfromhell.net/post/28206284910/hip-to-be-square

ComLuv

Homepage

http://comluv.com/

Copyblogger

Homepage

http://www.copyblogger.com/

10 Steps to Becoming a Better Writer (Poster), by Brian Clark

http://www.copyblogger.com/10-steps-to-better-writing/

The 11 "Secrets" of Prolific Content Creators

http://www.copyblogger.com/prolific-content-creation/

5 Simple Ways to Open Your Blog Post With a Bang, by Brian Clark

http://www.copyblogger.com/5-simple-ways-to-open-your-blog-post-with-a-bang/

The 7 Deadly Sins of Blogging, by Sonia Simone

http://www.copyblogger.com/blogging-sins/

A 7-Step Content Creator's Creativity Cleanse, by Jennifer Blanchard

http://www.copyblogger.com/content-creativity-cleanse/

Don't Read This or the Kitty Gets It! by Brian Clark

http://www.copyblogger.com/do-not-read-this-post-or-the-kitten-gets-it/

How to Create Better Content: Treat Your Readers Like Dogs, by Sonia Simone http://www.copyblogger.com/create-better-content/

How to Increase Your Blog Subscription Rate by 254%, by Willy Franzen

http://www.copyblogger.com/increase-blog-subscribers/

The Two Most Important Words in Blogging, by Brian Clark

http://www.copyblogger.com/the-two-most-important-words-in-blogging/

Cracked

Homepage

http://www.cracked.com/

The 5 Creepiest Urban Legends (That Happen to be True), by Nathan Birch

http://www.cracked.com/article_15628_the-5-creepiest-urban-legends-that-happen-to-be-true.html

Daily Kos

Homepage

http://www.dailykos.com/

Deadline

Homepage

http://www.deadline.com/hollywood/

Digg

Homepage

http://digg.com/

Disqus

Homepage

http://disqus.com/

Doug Neiner

Homepage

http://dougneiner.com/

DreamHost

Homepage

http://www.dreamhost.com/

Drudge Report

Homepage

http://www.drudgereport.com/

Drupal

Homepage

https://drupal.org/

Distributions

https://drupal.org/project/distributions

Drupal support

https://drupal.org/support

Installation guide

https://drupal.org/documentation/install

Recommended hosts

https://groups.drupal.org/node/234533

Theme gallery

https://drupal.org/project/themes

eBay

Homepage

http://www.ebay.com/

eHow

Homepage

http://www.ehow.com/

A Guide to Women's Athletic Wear, by Paula Carvajal

http://www.ehow.com/feature_12128320_guide-womens-athletic-wear.html

Etsy

Homepage

http://www.etsy.com/

Evernote

Homepage

http://evernote.com/

Facebook

Homepage

http://facebook.com/

FAIL Blog

Homepage

http://failblog.cheezburger.com/

Fuel Your Blogging

Homepage

http://www.fuelyourblogging.com/

Can Visitors See You In the Sidebar? – Feedback Friday, by Christopher Rice

http://www.fuelyourblogging.com/personal-image-sidebar/

The Hot List of Links for Bloggers, by Brandon Cox

http://www.fuelyourblogging.com/the-hot-list-of-links-for-bloggers-9/

How to Interview Absolutely Anybody, by Thomas Parnell

http://www.fuelyourblogging.com/how-to-interview-absolutely-anybody/

How to Make Writing Your Blog Posts Effortless, by James Chartrand

http://www.fuelyourblogging.com/how-to-make-writing-your-blog-posts-effortless/

How to Pitch Your Blog to Potential Advertisers, by Alex Denning

http://www.fuelyourblogging.com/how-to-pitch-your-blog-to-potential-advertisers/

If You're Blogging, Watch Your But, by Collin Elder

http://www.fuelyourblogging.com/if-youre-blogging-watch-your-but/

The Pros and Cons of Blogging Ahead, by Brandon Cox

http://www.fuelyourblogging.com/the-pros-and-cons-of-blogging-ahead/

The Pros and Cons of Blogging As You Go, by Brandon Cox

http://www.fuelyourblogging.com/the-pros-and-cons-of-blogging-as-you-go/

Revision: The Harsh – But Necessary – Literary Task Master, by Tom Chu

http://www.fuelyourblogging.com/revision-the-harsh-but-necessary-literary-task-master/

Should You Write Short or Long Blog Posts? by James Chartrand

http://www.fuelyourblogging.com/short-or-long-blog-posts/

What to Write for Your Very First Blog Post, by James Chartrand

http://www.fuelyourblogging.com/what-to-write-for-your-very-first-blog-post/

Getty Images

Homepage

http://www.gettyimages.ca/

Go Daddy

Homepage

http://ca.godaddy.com/

Goodreads

Homepage

http://www.goodreads.com/

Google

Google AdSense

http://google.com/adsense

Google AdWords

http://adwords.google.com/

Google AdWords – Keyword Tool

http://adwords.google.com/keywordplanner/

Google Alerts

http://google.com/alerts/

Google Analytics

http://google.com/analytics/

Google Docs

http://docs.google.com

Google Support – Blogger

https://support.google.com/blogger/

Google Webmaster Central Blog – More guidance on building high-quality sites

http://googlewebmastercentral.blogspot.ca/2011/05/more-guidance-on-building-high-quality.html

Hashtags.org

Homepage

http://www.hashtags.org/

Host Gator

Homepage

http://www.hostgator.com/

The Huffington Post

Homepage

http://www.huffingtonpost.com/

Jezebel

Homepage

http://jezebel.com/

Joystiq

Homepage

http://www.joystiq.com/

Kotaku

Homepage

http://kotaku.com/

L.A. Now

Homepage

http://www.latimes.com/local/lanow/

Laughing Squid

Blog homepage

http://laughingsquid.com/

Host homepage

https://laughingsquid.us/

Mail Chimp

Homepage

http://mailchimp.com/

Movable Type.com

Homepage

http://www.movabletype.com/

Movable Type.org

Homepage

http://movabletype.org/

Installation guide

http://movabletype.org/documentation/installation/

Movable Type forums

http://forums.movabletype.org/

Movable Type support

http://movabletype.org/support/

Server requirements

http://movabletype.org/documentation/beta/60/requirement.html

MyBlogGuest

Homepage

http://myblogguest.com/

Nuance

Dragon Speech Recognition Software

http://www.nuance.com/dragon/index.htm

The Official Google Blog

Homepage

http://googleblog.blogspot.com/

The New York Times

The Opinionator blog homepage

http://opinionator.blogs.nytimes.com/

The Morality of Migration, by Seyla Benhabib

http://opinionator.blogs.nytimes.com/2012/07/29/stone-immigration/?_r=0

PayPal

Homepage

https://www.paypal.com/ca/webapps/mpp/home

Perez Hilton

Homepage

http://perezhilton.com/

Pop Watch

Homepage

http://popwatch.ew.com/

ProBlogger

Homepage

http://www.problogger.net/

ReadWrite

Homepage

http://readwrite.com/

Reddit

Homepage

http://www.reddit.com/

RocketTheme

Drupal themes

http://www.rockettheme.com/drupal

WordPress.org themes

http://www.rockettheme.com/wordpress

SEOmoz

Title Tag

http://moz.com/learn/seo/title-tag

Seth Godin's Blog

Homepage

http://sethgodin.typepad.com/seths_blog/page/2/

Shawnblanc.net

Homepage

http://shawnblanc.net/

Answering Reader's Questions About Writing shawnblanc.net Full Time

http://shawnblanc.net/2011/05/reader-questions/

Blog Comments Are Like Cash

http://shawnblanc.net/2007/08/blog-comments-are-like-cash/

Comments (a lack-thereof)

http://shawnblanc.net/archive/

Mountain Lion Miscellany

http://shawnblanc.net/2012/07/mountain-lion-miscellany/

Shutterstock

Homepage

http://www.shutterstock.com/

Snopes

Baby Shoes

http://www.snopes.com/language/literary/babyshoes.asp

Stephenfry.com

Blog homepage

http://www.stephenfry.com/blog/

Mind Out

http://www.stephenfry.com/2011/09/21/mind-out/

StumbleUpon

Homepage

https://www.stumbleupon.com/return

Technorati

State of the Blogosphere 2011

http://technorati.com/social-media/article/state-of-the-blogosphere-2011-introduction/

Top 100 Blogs

http://technorati.com/blogs/top100/

Template Monster

Drupal Themes

http://www.templatemonster.com/drupal-themes.php

WordPress Themes

http://www.templatemonster.com/wordpress-themes.php

Theme Shark

Homepage

http://neptunethemes.com/

This isn't happiness

Homepage

http://thisisnthappiness.com/

TMZ

Homepage

http://www.tmz.com/

Towleroad News

Homepage

http://www.towleroad.com/

Typepad

Homepage

http://www.typepad.com/

Typepad Customer Center

http://everything.typepad.com/

The Unofficial Apple Weblog (TUAW)

Homepage

http://www.tuaw.com/

Venture Beat

Homepage

http://venturebeat.com/

Visual Teaching Alliance

Homepage

http://visualteachingalliance.com/

The White House Blog

Homepage

http://www.whitehouse.gov/blog

Wikipedia

Public Domain Image Resources

http://en.wikipedia.org/wiki/Wikipedia:Public_domain_image_resources

Wikiquote

Nathaniel Hawthorne

http://en.wikiquote.org/wiki/Nathaniel_Hawthorne

Wordle

Homepage

http://www.wordle.net/

WordPress.com

Homepage

http://wordpress.com/

WordPress.com Support

http://wordpress.com/support/

WordPress.org

Homepage

http://wordpress.org/

Installation guide

http://codex.wordpress.org/Installing_WordPress

Recommended hosts

http://wordpress.org/hosting/

Recommended themes

http://wordpress.org/themes/browse/top-rated/

Themes Directory

http://wordpress.org/themes/

WordPress.org support

http://en-ca.wordpress.org/support/

Xkcd

Homepage

http://xkcd.com/

Yahoo!

Yahoo! Answers

http://www.answers.yahoo.com/

YouTube

Homepage

http://www.youtube.com/

Zero Hedge

Homepage

http://www.zerohedge.com/

Print references

Part Three: Doing the Research

Keyword Research

Quotation from Mark Twain, from a letter to George Bainton, October 15, 1888. Printed in Bainton, George (ed.), *The art of authorship, advice to young beginners by leading authors.* London, 1890.

Part Four: Time to Write

Crafting a Headline

Paraphrased material from Bly, Robert W., The Copywriter's Handbook: A Step-By-Step Guide To Writing Copy That Sells, 3rd ed. New York: Henry Holt and Company, 2006.

Getting Personal

Paraphrased material from Andrews, Margaret, Sticky Readers: How to Attract a Loyal Blog Audience by Writing More Better. CreateSpace Independent Publishing Platform, 2011.

Connect with Scribendi.com online:

Twitter: http://twitter.com/Scribendi_Inc

Facebook: http://www.facebook.com/ScribendiInc

Scribendi.com's blog: http://www.scribendi.com/advice/

ABOUT THE AUTHOR

Scribendi.com was founded in 1997 as one of the world's first online editing and proofreading companies. Based in Ontario, Canada, the company's primary goal is to provide clients with fast, reliable, and affordable revision services. Today, Scribendi.com is the world's largest online proofreading and editing company.

Printed in Great Britain
by Amazon.co.uk, Ltd.,
Marston Gate.